COUNTRY DANCE
of Colonial America

JOHN FITZHUGH MILLAR

Thirteen Colonies Press

Williamsburg, Virginia

Library of Congress Cataloging-in-Publication Data

Millar, John Fitzhugh.
    Country dances of colonial America / John Fitzhugh Millar.
        p.   cm.
    Includes bibliographical references.
    ISBN 0-934943-29-X (hardback : acid-free) : $30.00. -- ISBN
0-934943-28-1 (paperback : acid-free) : $20.00
    1. Country dance--United States--History--18th century.
I. Title.
GV1623.M497 1990
793.3'4'0973--dc20   90-49922
                                                            CIP

This book is set primarily in Baskerville type. John Baskerville (1706-1775) devised this beautiful type in the 1750s in England and it remains unexcelled today. Benjamin Franklin was most enthusiastic about Baskerville's type designs, but they were not used in the U.S.A. until the end of the eighteenth century.

© Thirteen Colonies Press 1990
710 South Henry Street,
Williamsburg, Virginia, 23185 USA

Library of Congress Catalogue Number 90-49922
ISBN (USA)0-934943-28-1 paperback
            0-934943-29-X hardcover

TABLE OF CONTENTS

ABOUT THE AUTHOR

John Fitzhugh Millar received his AB from Harvard in 1966 and his MA in History from the College of William & Mary in 1981. He has spent a decade as a museum director in Newport, RI and has taught history at three colleges.He has devoted years to the study of various aspects of life in the eighteenth century, such as architecture, the decorative arts, classical & folk music, dance and ships, and has lectured extensively on these subjects. He was responsible for the construction of full-sized operational copies of the 24-gun sailing-frigate "Rose" (1756/1970) and the 12-gun sloop "Providence" (ca.1768/1976) and was in charge of the partial restoration of the 1733 Handel organ at Newport. He served for many years on the Rhode Island Bicentennial Commission and in 1970 he founded the Bicentennial Council of the Thirteen Original States, an organization that successfully raised millions of dollars to assist Bicentennial projects in the Thirteen States. He and his wife Cathy have recently built and furnished completely in period Newport House, a copy of a 1756 house that had been destroyed, and they run it as a Bed & Breakfast near the edge of Colonial Williamsburg. Country Dancing is held in the ballroom of Newport House every Tuesday evening. Millar's major published works include:

BUILDING EARLY AMERICAN WARSHIPS, 1988
CLASSICAL ARCHITECTURE IN RENAISSANCE EUROPE 1419–1585, 1987
EARLY AMERICAN SHIPS, 1986
ELIZABETHAN COUNTRY DANCES, 1986
A COMPLETE LIFE OF CHRIST, 1986
AMERICAN SHIPS OF THE COLONIAL & REVOLUTIONARY PERIODS, 1978
SHIPS OF THE AMERICAN REVOLUTION, 1976
RHODE ISLAND: FORGOTTEN LEADER OF THE REVOLUTIONARY ERA, 1975
COLONIAL & REVOLUTIONARY WAR SEA SONGS & CHANTEYS, 1975
THE ARCHITECTS OF THE AMERICAN COLONIES, 1968

ACKNOWLEDGEMENTS

Before anything else, I offer my sincerest apologies to all those readers who had expected this book to appear some time in 1988. My original plan had been to have the book out some time in 1988 to mark the 200th anniversary of John Griffiths' dance book published at Providence, the oldest American dance publication that survives.

Alas, the book is about two years late, thanks in part to my unfamiliarity with my computer-word processor, which managed to lose the entire text of the book for good. Another reason for the delay has been that we have recently built Newport House, a reproduction of a 1756 house designed by Peter Harrison that had been torn down, and we are now running it as a Bed & Breakfast; I never thought that so much time could be taken up with scrubbing bathrooms, but that was all time not available for producing the book. On the bright side, as happens with all books, the longer one waits before publication, the more useful and accurate the information that one can put in it; in addition, Newport House contains a fine, large, ballroom, where the Williamsburg Heritage Dancers do English and American country dances every Tuesday evening and the Williamsburg Scottish Dancers do Scottish country dances every Thursday evening; this took me a long time to complete, but the dancing makes it all worth while, and we hope that whenever you readers travel through the Williamsburg area you will come and join us for dancing.

I also owe you readers a further apology that the title of the book is a trifle misleading. The words "Colonial America" may be thought of as referring to anything prior to 1776, or 1783 (the end of the War of Independence) or possibly 1790 (the date when the last of the thirteen original states ratified the Constitution), and I truly thought that the dances in the book would all predate 1790, but I put up very little resistance when a handful of dances published between 1790 and 1800 (but possibly written earlier) found their way into the book. I hope the book contains enough genuine dances of the colonial period to satisfy all readers.

No book of this kind is ever written in a vacuum, and whatever I have done merely stands on the shoulders of the many better people who have worked at this subject before and continue to do so. I owe particular thanks to George Fogg of Boston, who first taught me country dancing in the 1970s and made it fun; to Leland "Lee" and Gail Ticknor, who founded and for so long nurtured the Williamsburg Heritage Dancers and who taught me to look at dance from an historical perspective; to Kate "Kitty" and Bob Keller, who have done more for the study of historical early American dance and popular music than anyone else; and to my friend Al Klyberg, Director of the Rhode Island Historical Society, for so kindly giving permission for the publication of a facsimile of the Griffiths book, the sole surviving copy of which resides in their collections.

I am grateful for help received from the American Antiquarian Society; from the Public Archives of Canada; from the Country Dance & Song Society at 17 New South Street, Northampton, MA, 01062; from the English Folk Dance & Song Society at Cecil Sharp House, 2 Regent's Park Road, London, NW1 7AY; and from the Royal Scottish Country Dance Society at 12 Coates Crescent, Edinburgh, EH3 7AF, Scotland. I give the addresses (as of 1990) of these societies because I hope that readers will be moved to join these organizations and support financially the fine work they are doing.

Particular thanks to Gail Ticknor for her assistance in completing the tune incipits for many of the tunes in the Trois Rivieres manuscript book from Canada (ca.1765). No doubt, the original tunes were completed somewhat differently, but until the original tunes can be loacted I think it is better to complete them as carefully as we can so that they can be included in this book for the enjoyment of dancers.

I am full of gratitude to many other people who have shared information with me that has helped with this book, and I hope I am not omitting too many in this alphabetical listing: Dr. Anthony Barrand; Gene Bjerke; Dr. George Emmerson; Merry Feyock; Mae Fraley; James Fuld; Rich Galloway; Jack Gardner; Capt. Miles Hamby; Christine Helwig; Cyril "Chip" Hendrickson; Fried Herman; Christopher Hogwood; Bob Kassebaum; Jim Morrison; Dorothy Poucher; John & Lynn Symborski; Lou Vosteen; Paul Vosteen; Herb Watson, Jr.; and Howard H Way, Jr. I hope they will not be disappointed with the book.

Finally, I am profoundly grateful to my graceful wife and dance partner, Cathy. Shortly after we were married, when I had established myself as some sort of authority on eighteenth-century architecture, decorative arts, ships, clothing and folk & classical music, it was she who pointed out that no eighteenth-century person was complete without the dance of the period, so she dragged me off to a class offered by George Fogg and we never looked back after that. Cathy has been very patient with me while this book has been under way, and so I dedicate the book to her.

Finally, if you are already a country dancer, keep dancing! If you are not, I urge you to start. The Country Dance & Song Society has programs to help you start a group in your area and they can send experts to teach your group in a workshop; for that matter, when I am not scrubbing too many bathrooms, Cathy and I are available to run a workshop for your dance group, so we look forward to hearing from you.

John Fitzhugh Millar   Newport House, Williamsburg, Virginia, 1990.

HISTORICAL BACKGROUND

Throughout the colonial period in America, country dancing was the principal recreation of all social classes, rather equivalent to watching television plus playing golf and tennis today. Americans had inherited this tendency from Elizabethan England, and many continental Europeans as well picked up English country dancing as their own.

In Elizabethan England, several distinct dance forms flourished side by side. Traditional ritual dances, whose origins are thought by some to go back perhaps as far as the Druid era (not likely), were danced in the countryside on special occasions. Ancient ritual dances that survive to our own day include the Abbots Bromley Horn Dance from Staffordshire, the Padstow Mayers' Hobby-horse Dance from Cornwall and the Helston Furry Dance also from Cornwall.

Until recently, it was widely believed that Morris dances were ancient ritual dances, but recent research tends to show that they were not. Morris dances apparently were different things in different places, perhaps more of an occasion than a specific dance. Morris dancing included country dancing and also entertainment between the acts on the theatre stage beginning some time in the fifteenth century. The word Morris derives from the Spanish word Morisco, meaning Moorish, because dancers blackened their faces to resemble Africans from Morocco. English and American Puritans in the mid-seventeenth century outlawed both theatre and its accompanying Morris dance, and when Morris was revived a generation later (perhaps in altered form) no one could remember exactly what had been the traditions of its origins. Morris has undoubtedly been changed over the years and was once more or less identical to country dancing.

In 1578, Sir Walter Ralegh's (yes, that's the way he spelled his name) ship Falcon was separated from the rest of his fleet of ten ships. He intended to explore the coast of North Carolina and the Chesapeake region for a possible settlement before proceeding to Newfoundland and thence home again. However, the ship never reached America because he decided to turn back when the crew ran out of wine in mid-Atlantic! In a deposition in a lawsuit relating to the voyage, Fernandes the pilot stated that among the goods aboard the ship (which may have been used to purchase more wine in the Canary Islands) were "certain morys belles" (certain Morris bells)—part of a Morris dancer's attire. Morris actually reached America only a few years later in 1583 in Sir Humphrey Gilbert's expedition to reclaim Newfoundland for English possession. Captain Edward Hayes of the ship Golden Hinde reported: "Ashore the morris dancers, hobby horse, and jack o'greens cavorted, to the delight of the fishermen, many of whom joined in . . .."

Another form of dancing current in Elizabethan England was what is loosely called Court dance. Much court dance was intricate, elaborate and energetic, and it was confined almost exclusively to the nobility. One of the theories behind it (apparently originating in France) was that it needed to be difficult because then anyone who was able to master it could prove that he had absolutely nothing else to do but practise dancing, which mean of course that he was therefore one of the nobility. Court dances, which included the Coranto, the Almain, the Pavan, the "lascivious" Lavolta and, most impressive of all, the Galliard, were, like the much later Minuet, danced by one couple at a time, either alone or in a procession, who did not interact with others. The directions for quite a few of these dances survive in a number of places, including a handful of English manuscripts (mostly between 1570 and 1670), and in a remarkable French book of 1589, Orchesographie by Thoinot Arbeau (anagrammatic pen-name for Jehan Tabourot), of which a modern paperback edition has been published by Dover.

Queen Elizabeth took a keen interest in dancing, and was not alone among European rulers in choosing her advisors from among good dancers; Sir Christopher Hatton is said to have received his post as Lord Chancellor as a result of his dancing abilities. Elizabeth continued her own dancing to the end of her long life; the Spanish ambassador disapprovingly reported that "the head of the Church of England and Ireland" danced three or four strenuous galliards at the age of 65 at the Twelfth Night Revels of 1599. However, in 1661, the young King Louis XIV of France, who loved dancing, realised that it was in his best interest to keep his skillful dancers separate from his skilled government policy advisors, so he founded the Academie Royale de Danse, the beginning of professional ballet. His advisors, thus deprived of participating in the ever more difficult steps of the court dancing that was now in the hands of the professional dancers, turned at least part of their attention to what was already popular in England, English Country Dancing.

Whereas court dancing was intended mainly for one couple at a time to show off that they had been rigorously trained in the elaborate footwork required, country dancing was for couples in groups or sets of two or more, using relatively simple steps to trace patterns and figures over the ground and interacting with the other dancers of the set. Melusine Wood traces the roots of English country dancing to the troubadours who lived in Provence in what is now the south of France, and who were driven out by the savage massacres by the Pope's forces in their crusade against the Albigensian heresy, beginning in 1208. Many of these refugees found shelter in distant England, where the dance tradition they started there was permitted to develop almost in isolation from the rest of the world. By the time of Henry VIII (reigned 1509–1547), their farandole dances had evolved into forms recognizable today, including Dargason, Sellenger's Round, Half Hannikin and Trenchmore.

It is believed that Elizabeth was interested mainly in court dance until 1591, when she visited Lord and Lady Montague at Cowdray House in Sussex and watched her hosts doing country dances with their tenants and servants. From that moment on, country dance appears frequently in the records of entertainment at court. Presumably, some new country dances were composed to be used at court, because in 1600 the Maids of Honour were reported to be dancing both "the old and the new country dances." It is possible that the old dances meant those most suited for outdoor use, the circles and longways sets for as many as will, and the new dances were the small sets best suited for small rooms in the house; certainly, the long galleries that were the hallmark of the largest Elizabethan houses were well suited to longways sets for as many as will.

The popularity of country dancing at court continued during the reigns of James I and Charles I and even through the supposedly austere Puritan Commonwealth. From at least 1471 onwards, records exist of Morris, court and country dances being done by the young gentlemen of the Inns of Court (in the United States, the closest counterpart to the Inns of Court would be a law school). A few manuscript directions for country dances survive from the 1640s, but none was published until 1651. For a selection of early country dances, see the author's Elizabethan Country Dances (Thirteen Colonies Press, 1986).

In 1651, when Puritan power in England was at its height, publisher John Playford issued a book, The English Dancing Master: or Plaine and easie Rules for the Dancing of Country Dances, with the Tune to each Dance. It is important to note that Playford himself probably did not write any of the dances, but merely served as publisher. Experts feel they can detect the writing styles of six or eight different contributors, some of whom were merely putting into print dances that had been around for years, while others may have composed dances especially for the book. A fair number of typographical errors have caused some confusion in interpreting some of the dance instructions, but for the most part the directions are remarkably clear. It seems that the books were not intended for the general public of a later era but rather for people who already knew the dances and needed only a quick reminder from a book.

Playford's shop was next to the Temple Church at one of the Inns of Court, which meant that his dance books had a ready market in all the law students who had to pass his door on their way to and from studies. In fact, it is believed that Playford had been asked to publish the book specifically for the use of the law students, who were expected to find dancing good for their posture and manners. The book, which contains 105 dances, was so popular that Playford brought out further editions with new (and newly-collected old) dances, and the series was continued long after Playford's death by his son Henry Playford and his successor John Young. Depending on how they are counted, a total of about 27 editions were published until about 1727 (some had no date printed on them). Surprisingly, many dances that can be traced back independently to the Elizabethan era turn up for the first time in print only in the later editions of Playford, sometimes more than a century after the first recorded reference to the title. This suggests that some dances remained popular for long periods of time.

The first rivals to Playford's books began appearing early in the eighteenth century, such as For the Further Improvement of Dancing by RaoulAugerFeuillet and John Essex in 1710, Country Dances by Thomas Bray, 1699, and Twenty Four New Country Dances for the Year 1710 by J. Walsh and P. Randall in 1709. Dozens of further books appeared throughout the eighteenth century and beyond by the likes of Kynaston, Wright, Neal, Johnson, Rutherford, Thompson, Bride, Fishar, Gallini, Longman, Skillern, Cantelo, Preston and Dodd, among others.

By the eighteenth century, subtle changes began to appear in country dance. Where dance directions had once been for Men and Women, the Georgian dance books were written for Gentlemen and Ladies. All that really meant was that in the earlier period, all social classes might have been seen in the same room or even in the same set, duchess and scullery maid alike, but in the eighteenth century the different social classes generally held their country dance assemblies separately.

Around the beginning of the eighteenth century, the great variety of dance formations known in earlier years in England (such as the circle for as many as will, the square for four couples and the square for two couples, the circle for three couples and most longways dances for three couples) had dwindled to three: the duple-minor progressive longways for as many as will and occasionally the three-couple longways set, plus a newcomer, the triple-minor progressive longways for as many as will. Some additional variety was offered to the well-to-do by a proliferation of dancing-masters (a small percentage of whom were immigrants from France, perhaps as a result of the persecution of the Protestants following the revocation of the Edict of Nantes), who tried with only limited success to introduce what we now call baroque and French court dance steps, such as the minuet step, the bourree and the contretemps. Perhaps the instructors felt that trying to invent a demand for complicated and exotic steps was the best way to ensure that they would have relatively steady employment. This kind of snob-appeal had the best chance of working among some of the wealthy, who may have felt a need to prove to the world that they had no need to earn a living, and thus could afford the time required to learn and practise the steps, but the best evidence indicates that complicated steps were the exception rather than the rule.

Another development that arrived in England from France, about 1760, was the popular return of the four-couple square sets that had been invented in Elizabethan England, exported to France in the 1660s and forgotten in England some time after 1700. The French called these dances Cotillons, which was anglicized to Cotillions. Cotillions consisted of any of over a dozen well-known verses or "changes," each followed by a chorus or "figure" that was peculiar to that particular dance. A somewhat similar dance was called the Quadrille in the nineteenth century.

Folklorist Cecil Sharp and other commentators have noticed a decline in quality of the average written country dance dating from the end of Playford's life, and that decline was especially marked in the early nineteenth century (perhaps connected to the sudden surge of complicated steps from

1792 onwards, reflecting the large number of French refugees fleeing the French Revolution, who tried to find work in Britain and America doing the only thing they knew, teaching complicated dance steps). At that time, country dances seem to have lost their appeal with the upper classes in the face of the challenge from new couple-dances, such as the Viennese Waltz and later the Polka (even though the couple-dances of a century earlier, such as the Minuet, the Gavotte and the Allemande, had made very little headway against the country dance). By 1900, the only country dance still danced regularly by the English upper classes was Sir Roger de Coverley, which was often used to close an evening of dancing couple-dances, and in America a similar dance, the Virginia Reel, filled the same need; both are variations on the sixteenth-century country dance Trenchmore.

But country dancing remained alive, if altered, outside the upper classes. In England, the country folk continued the form, although nearly all of their actual dances were of recent composition. In America, country dances had accompanied the settlers on their expansion into the west, but these had been forced to leave behind both dance masters and dance books, with the result that the dance forms underwent some changes over the years, partially in response to their different environment. In the relatively remote communities of New England, like Vermont's Green Mountains, both square and longways formations survived, the latter under the name of Contras. When the French had first picked up English country dances, they called them Contrée-danses, using the ancient French cognate word Contrée, which later got shortened by usage to Contre (without the accent), which sounded like Contra to the Americans. Although it may seem natural to call a dance that had lines of people opposite each other a Contra dance (after the Latin word, Contra, meaning against or opposite) that was not the way in which the word developed, contrary to what contradancers often say. In fact, to the French, the term Contredanse as often as not meant a square formation rather than a longways set, which means that the lovely tunes written by Mozart and others of his era and called Contredanses were in fact for square dances—a far cry from the kind of music normally used to accompany modern square dances!

Further west, only the square formations survived, but so transformed as to be scarcely recognizable. Apart from the addition of a plethora of newly-invented figures, western square dances depend entirely on a caller for instructions delivered with split-second timing, and the figures are not necessarily danced to the phrases of the music (the music is somewhat irrelevant, and thus can take almost any form). The new square dance form, however, had enough power to spread around the globe. The irony was complete during and just after World War II when the then Princess Elizabeth actively encouraged the English to pick up the western square dance newly imported to England by American troops.

At the end of the nineteenth century, a remarkable movement began that is still developing today, a movement that can best be called a revival, for it was concerned with reviving certain historical forms of architecture, folk-song, country dance, musical instruments and music to be played on ancient musical instruments (or at least on instruments made and played according to historical principles). Ahead of the movement was William Chappell, with his 1859 book, Popular Music of the Olden Time. Possibly the first of the musical revivalists was Arnold Dolmetsch, who, at the same time as he had been appointed to teach violin at the Royal Academy of Music in London in the 1880s, discovered and purchased a recorder and a rebec, two ancient instruments that had been completely forgotten by his day. Dolmetsch, working in both England and the United States, soon began to make copies of these and many other early instruments, and to experiment with various techniques of playing them. Much later, his wife Mabel concerned herself with early dances and their music.

Dolmetsch's work came to the attention of composer Ralph Vaughan-Williams and folklorist Cecil Sharp (1859–1924). Folk dances of many countries were being revived at that time, but no one in a position to write about them knew that England even had any distinct forms of ancient dance. Then Sharp, inspired by Dolmetsch, became so interested in discovering English dances that he researched and published a book on Morris dance in 1905 and followed that with a series of six books on country dance starting about 1910. The Sharp books contained a mixture of traditional dances he had observed in the countrysides of England and America and other dances he had culled from various Playford editions and re-interpreted for modern readers.

Sharp's English country dances achieved instant popularity in England and the United States, both

4

among adults and in the school systems. In America, Dr. Luther H. Gulick had already paved the way by introducing international folk dancing to the New York school system in 1903.

Sharp's books have run through many reprints and have become mainstays of dancing sponsored by the English Folk Dance & Song Society in Britain and the Country Dance & Song Society in the United States and Canada, and many other groups around the world. Sharp was generally scrupulous in researching and interpreting his material, but he was occasionally forced to guess what was intended by a term in Playford, and subsequent research by Sharp himself and by others, including the late Patrick Shuldham-Shaw, has proved that he sometimes guessed wrong (as in the case of the dance term "siding").

Dr. Jean C. Milligan was so impressed by Sharp's accomplishments for English dance that she decided to attempt the same sort of reconstruction for Scottish Country Dance in the 1920s, but her research was unfortunately far less thorough than Sharp's, with the result that Scottish country dances, which two centuries ago were virtually indistinguishable from English country dances, are now a totally different field. Moreover, Dr. Milligan's interpretations have now been cast in stone under the authority of the Royal Scottish Country Dance Society, which she founded. To be fair, the history of Scottish dance can be a little confusing, especially in view of the fact that the Scots had their own indigenous country dance (the four-some reels, which generally consisted of a series of reels or heys interspersed with setting steps and possibly turns, but nothing more) and they also had their own versions of English country dance, imported from south of the border.

Whatever distortions Dr. Milligan may have wrought to Scottish historical dancing, it was nothing when compared to what Irish "experts" did in altering the historical country dances of their country, but perhaps their zeal was inspired in part by the Irish independence movement, which was in full swing at that time.

At the time that Sharp issued his books, many people in England, perhaps disillusioned with the heavy industrialization and materialism of the day, expressed a romantic nostalgia for the simpler life of Merrie England, which they felt could be recreated in part by reviving ancient folk traditions (hence the Arts and Crafts movement of William Morris), such as folk-dancing on the village greens. Accordingly, country dance experienced a tremendous revival for a short time, but the idea fell apart in the face of the onslaught of the First World War. After the war, country dancing was for a time largely confined to the school systems (hence the large number of older people whose eyes brighten as they say, "Oh yes, we used to do that in school, but I've forgotten all about it since then.") until released by the next great folk revival following World War II. That folk revival of the 1950s, in its turn, seems to have inspired a new interest in ancient musical performance techniques, and the result of that spate of research has been the proliferation of early music orchestras led by the likes of Christopher Hogwood, John E. Gardiner, Trevor Pinnock and many others whose names are fast becoming household words; Dolmetsch (whose family carries on his traditions) would have been proud of what he began, even if a little bewildered.

Here a few words should be said about the music that accompanies country dancing. Unlike modern squares and contras, which can and do use almost any music to hand, historical country dances are generally danced to music that is specific to the particular dance. Thus, for experienced dancers, the old axiom, "the music will tell you what to do," can be entirely accurate. On the other hand, even in Playford's day, an alternate tune was occasionally substituted, and Sharp and subsequent writers have done likewise.

Many country dance tunes also had words. In some cases, song-tunes were borrowed for dancing (but generally played too fast for singing), but doubtless other tunes that were written for dancing acquired words at a later date.

Whereas Haydn, Mozart, Beethoven, Schubert and many other leading composers in continental Europe wrote contredanse tunes, most of the outstanding tunes for English country dances are anonymous. A handful of them can be traced to Purcell, Handel, Thomas Arne (composer of "Rule, Britannia"), Henry Carey (composer of "God Save the King") and to various dancing masters, but the vast majority can not be attributed to any known composer. Nonetheless, the merit and quality of these anonymous melodies has frequently been recognized by the inclusion of many of them in concerts and

5

recordings not intended for accompanying dancing. Indeed, the author would not be surprised if many non-dancers acquired this book for its musical content alone.

As mentioned above, Morris dancing was reported in America as early as the sixteenth century. It is likely that country dancing arrived at more or less the same time, and may have been danced in Newfoundland, the fishing communities on the islands off the coast of Maine and the Roanoke Island colony of Sir Walter Ralegh in North Carolina (1585–9), but no specific record of dancing in these places has yet been found. Even at Jamestown, Virginia (founded 1607), the only documented connection to country dance is the arrival there about 1618 of Thomas Lanier, a court musician of James I. Did Lanier also teach dancing?

The first solid references to country dance in America come from half a century after Lanier. Charles Cheate taught dancing in Virginia around 1670 and moved to Boston in 1676. He was not the first in Boston, for an anonymous dance teacher was recorded there in 1672. Two dance teachers were driven out of Boston for reasons not connected with dance, Henri Sherlot in 1681 and Francis Stepney in 1685. By 1706, proper dance academies were well established in Boston and Philadelphia, and probably many other places as well.

Dance teachers came from varied backgrounds. Edward Enstone was the respected organist of King's Chapel, Boston in 1716. Stephen Tenoe, a minor composer of art songs, taught dance while he was an indentured servant in Virginia in 1739.

Peter Pelham, a church organist and composer in Boston, Newport, New York, Philadelphia, Williamsburg and Charleston, was related to the British Prime Minister. Teaching dance was one occupation that was unquestionably open to women. For example, in Williamsburg, at least three women are known to have made their living teaching dance: Sarah Hallam (ex-actress), Barbara the Baroness de Graffenriedt, and Mary Stagg. A surprisingly small percentage of dance masters in America were French, according to the research of Kate Keller, but one Frenchman, Monsieur Violet, successfully taught country dance to the Iroquois Indians, who solemnly paid him for his trouble with beaver skins and cured bear meat!

Another Frenchman, Alexandre-Marie Quesnay the Chevalier de Beaurepaire, arrived in 1777 to fight under Washington, but quickly thought better of it and began establishing a chain of schools to teach dance and culture in Virginia, Philadelphia, New York and New England; a certain B. C. Quesnet teaching in Philadelphia in 1799 is likely to have been his brother, given the lack of standardized spelling in those days. John Griffiths, who worked for a time in Quesnay's schools, was one of the most notable of the dancing masters. Not only did he teach in New York City, New Haven, Hartford, Wethersfield, Norwich, Litchfield, Providence, Newport, Boston, Northampton, other New England communities and possibly in South Carolina, but he was also the first to get a book of dances published in America. His first book was apparently published in New Haven in 1786, but all copies of it have been lost. His next dance book was published in Providence in 1788 (with his name spelled wrong!) and only a single original copy survives at the Rhode Island Historical Society; a facsimile has been included in this book, thanks to the generosity of the Rhode Island Historical Society. A detailed study of Griffiths, John Griffiths, Eighteenth-Century Itinerant Dancing Master, by Kate Keller has been published by the Hendrickson Group in Connecticut.

Then, as now, dancing had a variety of purposes. Dances with fancy footwork, such as the minuet, were designed to show social distinctions, for only people of leisure could theoretically spend the time necessary to learn the complicated steps well enough to perform in public. Country dances, by contrast, could be danced by any able-bodied person of any social class and practically any age. Young people were started out learning to dance because it taught them good posture, elegance of body movement and social graces.

In seventeenth-century New England at least, young people were taught country dance only with members of their own sex, and in the early days anyone who tried to do differently was liable to encounter trouble. For example, in the 1630s, some renegades were accused of running a licentious settlement at Wollaston, Massachusetts called Merry Mount, about mid-way between those centers of rectitude, Boston and Plymouth. These jolly folk are known to have danced around a large maypole before they were driven out by their starchy neighbors and the maypole cut down. About fifty years later, a maypole was indignantly cut down in Charlestown, MA in 1687, but it was replaced by an even larger one, to the great discomfiture of the diarist, Judge Sewall. Incidentally, although it is fashionable for English folklorists to state that English (and hence American as well) maypoles never had streamers dangling from the top to be woven by the dancers as they danced a hey around the pole, at least one mid-eighteenth-century English engraving (after a now-lost painting by Canaletto) proves them wrong. Therefore, the exact form of the Wollaston and Charlestown maypoles (or any other early American maypoles) can not be known with certainty.

Puritan reaction to country dancing was predictably mixed. Some clergy thundered against dancing of any kind, whereas others encouraged it (as long as the dancers did nothing the slightest bit lewd or lascivious). A favorite activity, for instance, among the New England Congregationalists was the holding of an Ordination Ball to celebrate the addition of new clergy; the earliest of these for which we have a specific record was that in honor of the Reverend Timothy Edwards in 1694 in Massachusetts. Even such a staunch Puritan divine as the Reverend John Cotton wrote that he approved of country dancing, "yea, tho' mixt," whereas both Increase Mather and Cotton Mather preferred it "unmixt." The latter was particularly annoyed by a country dance ball held on Christmas Day in 1711, although such balls had long been a traditional way of celebrating Christmas—a tradition carried on today in the author's house most years.

Of course, another important reason for the popularity of country dancing (to the obvious chagrin of some of the Puritans) was to meet people of the opposite sex. According to eighteenth-century etiquette, one was not supposed to speak to anyone to whom one had not been formally introduced by a third party, but an important crack in this monolithic rule was that one could freely converse with anyone who had ever danced in the same set. It is said that the popularity of triple-minor dances reflects the time the third couples could spend chatting or flirting during the dance.

It seems, though, that dancers in the eighteenth century frequently encountered a problem well known to most organizers of country dance balls today, that of the gender balance. We are told of a ball in Virginia in 1774 attended by 70 people, but they were 41 women and 29 men. Even worse, it is likely that a third of those men quickly retired to a back room for some serious drinking and gambling at cards, leaving about twice as many women as men on the dance floor. Thus, women were often forced to dance with other women, for that was more likely to bring them to the attention of the few dancing men than playing wallflower. George Washington noted "256 elegantly dressed and handsome ladies" attending a ball in his honor in 1791 at the Exchange Building in Charleston, but a simple look at the room today is enough to show that insufficient space existed for an equal number of men at the ball there.

Not much has been said about still another reason for country dancing, but it undoubtedly was a major factor in the days before central heating. Fireplaces were and are notoriously poor ways to heat a room; right in front of the hearth the heat can be intense and yet a mere ten feet away ice can be forming in a container of water. However, half an hour of spirited country dancing is a proven way of bringing a cold room or even an entire house up to a comfortable temperature, and this may be why some people in eighteenth-century America danced nearly every evening in the winter. It may also explain why many (but by no means all) pictures of country dancing in the seventeenth and eighteenth centuries show the men wearing their hats, since the most efficient way to keep a body warm is to cover the top of the head.

Modern American country dancers dance chiefly because it is fun, and their early American ancestors would no doubt have agreed with them. Philip Fithian noted in his diary in Virginia in 1774 that one of his friends was worried lest the weather prevent people from turning out for his ball, but "blow high, blow low, he need not be afraid; Virginians are of genuine Blood—They will dance or die!"

Monsieur de Sales, a French commentator visiting Canada in the 1770s, wrote: "I've never known a nation loving dancing more than the Canadians. They still do French cotillions and minuets, which they intersperse with English country dances." Some two decades later, and English visitor to Canada wrote that dancing was the ruling passion of the Canadians.

Moreau de Saint-Méry, a French visitor to Philadelphia about 1795, who was used to the rigorously difficult footwork associated with dancing in French society, expressed surprise at how much Americans enjoyed dancing: "All American girls or women are fond of dancing, which is one of their greatest pleasures. The men like it almost as much. They indulge in this pleasure, either in the morning, from eight to eleven, or in the evening from the end of the day far into the night . . . Dancing, for the inhabitants of the United States, is less a matter of self-display than it is of true enjoyment. At the same dance you will see a grandfather, his son and his grandson, but more often still the grandmother, her daughter and the granddaughter. If a Frenchman comments upon this with surprise, he is told that each one dances for his own amusement, and not because it's the thing to do." Saint-Méry's positive view was partially offset by the Reverend Andrew Burnaby, a mid-eighteenth-century visitor from England, who proclaimed that Americans were "immoderately fond of dancing," and of course by this he meant country dancing.

Most balls and assemblies in early America were indoors, although descriptions exist of outdoors dances. For example, on May Day in 1727, many people participated in festivities outdoors at Jamestown, VA, which involved selecting the Queen of the May, dancing around the maypole, a fiddlers' contest and general dancing on the green.

At indoor balls and assemblies, the typical pattern was for the event to start with a few minuets, one couple at a time in strict order of rank or social standing. For those who did not care for the minuet, there might be a short period for dancing solo jigs or hornpipes, followed by another short period of reels (generally Scottish dances for two couples at a time and/or "Virginia" dances for three couples at a time or occasionally more). Finally came the country dances, usually for several hours and lasting well past midnight.

Since country dancing was for all social classes, many types of buildings were employed to hold dances. The wealthiest people would have a suitable room in their houses, sometimes the upstairs stair hall. Some assemblies were held at statehouses or courthouses or market buildings or in purpose-built dance-assembly halls. Others were held at taverns, there being many different classes of taverns to suit the social standing of the patrons.

In Canada, no less than everywhere else, dances were held in almost every community, but the largest balls were at Montreal and Halifax. Balls were even held in the new Loyalist communities in Ontario within a few months of their being settled after the War of Independence. At Montreal, the Marquis de Vaudreuil's mansion, from which he ran the regional government, had a splendid ballroom, but the house has long since disappeared. Haldimand House, near Quebec City, was one of the headquarters of the young Duke of Kent in the 1790s, and many balls were held there; it is now a nursing home.

In New Hampshire, some of the finest eighteenth-century Portsmouth mansions have elegant rooms that were intended for dancing. Governor Sir John Wentworth had the famous architect Peter Harrison design him a fabulous mansion with a large ballroom in 1767 in the remote community of Wolfeborough, but the mansion was destroyed years ago. Wentworth advertised that he required two footmen, who could also play the French horn for dances.

In Puritan Boston, where as early as 1713 a ball given by Governor Joseph Dudley was reported to being still going strong past three in the morning, some assemblies were held at the DeBlois Concert Hall and others above the market in the original Faneuil Hall (an early work of Peter Harrison, who appointed the painter John Smibert to oversee construction in his absence). One of the finest ballrooms was undoubtedly at Governor Shirley's Shirley Place, built in then-rural Roxbury to designs by Peter Harrison in 1746; it had a musicians' gallery. The house still stands, but so greatly altered as to be unrecognizable.

Newport, fifth largest city in British America, was the principal center of culture for Rhode Island, with Providence a distant second. At the "Turtle Frolic" ball at Newport just before Christmas, 1752 (so called because Samuel Freebody hosted the event at Fort George on Goat Island in Newport Harbor and donated copious amounts of turtle soup cooked by Captain Jahleel Brenton's African chef with the improbable name of Cuffy Cockroach) three of the dances danced are recorded, the earliest such record; they were Arcadian Nuptials, Pease Straw and The Faithful Shepherd, the directions for two of which were not published, even in England, until many years later. Another record tells of a ballroom at Newport in 1756 for common sailors, under the ownership of one Lindee. "At this place all kinds of dissipation, licentiousness and obscenity were practised; one piece of amusement invented by the sailors was to make up a purse for the winner of a foot race between two girls, who were to run under cover of their under garment only . . ."

In addition to dance assembly rooms on Mary Street (now destroyed) Newport had two buildings designed for dancing. Peter Harrison designed the Brick Market in the 1760s, and the French officers stationed in Newport in 1780–1 built a ballroom for their exclusive use on Clarke Street, which still stands in altered form as a house. When George Washington visited the French in 1781, they gave a grand ball for him at the 1738 statehouse, and the diary of Peggy Champlin records many details of that ball. Newport was also the home of Newport Gardner, an African who was brought there as a 14-year-old slave in 1760, and who so quickly mastered English reading and writing and western music that dances and tunes attributed to him were published in England only a few years later.

New Haven and New London, both places visited by dance master John Griffiths, were the two major communities in Connecticut. At least two taverns survive in Connecticut with upstairs walls that can be hinged up to make two or three bedrooms into a single large ballroom, the Keeler Tavern in Ridgefield (1772) and the Pomeroy Stage House at Coventry (1801).

In New York City, only two buildings survive where balls were held in the eighteenth century: Fraunces Tavern (now much altered) and the Morris Mansion (much enlarged in the nineteenth century), the latter the product of a collaboration between architects Peter Harrison and John Edward Prior.

John Edward Prior designed three of New Jersey's finest houses where balls were held. Lord Stirling's estate at Basking Ridge has now been destroyed, and the Proprietary House (Governor's Mansion) at Perth Amboy has been greatly altered, but the Ford Mansion at Morristown, where George Washington had his headquarters, has been restored and is open to the public, thanks to the National Park Service.

Quakers were generally opposed to dancing, so few of the earliest buildings in Philadelphia were used for dancing, other than the Long Gallery upstairs at the statehouse (now called Independence Hall). By the second half of the eighteenth century, however, many of the largest houses, such as Mount Pleasant and Cliveden (both open to the public) were built for Episcopalians, and balls were frequently held there. Peter Harrison designed Walnut Grove for a Quaker family in the late 1740s, but it was taken over by the British as their headquarters during their occupation of Philadelphia and was the scene of the celebrated "Mischianza" ball on 18 May, 1778; the house disappeared years ago.

Delaware was similarly dominated by Quakers, but balls were held there in private houses and in the new statehouse at Dover, built just after the War of Independence.

Annapolis was the principal city of colonial Maryland and was the site for numerous balls, including some sponsored by the Tuesday Club (some of whose members composed excellent chamber music somewhat in the style of Handel). In the 1760s the citizens organized the construction of a large hall specifically for dance assemblies; the building still stands in greatly altered form and is now used for city government. Fine ballrooms were planned for two governors' mansions designed by Peter Harrison in the 1740s, Belair for retiring Governor Ogle, near Bowie (the city of Bowie owns the house and intends to use it for receptions), and a mansion in Annapolis for incoming Governor Bladen, now greatly altered and used by Saint John's College as MacDowell Hall. The Hammond-Harwood House, designed by William Buckland in 1774, has a fine ballroom.

The principal cities of colonial Virginia were Norfolk (sixth largest in British America) and Williamsburg, the seat of government. Norfolk was burned by American troops in the Revolution, so no dance rooms survive there, but at Williamsburg visitors can see where dancing was held at the Governor's Palace, the statehouse (called the Capitol), the Raleigh Tavern and Wetherburn's Tavern. At Alexandria, Gadsby's Tavern (designed by John Ariss) has no fewer than two eighteenth-century ballrooms, in which George Washington is known to have danced, when he was not dancing in the large ballroom he built onto his mansion, Mount Vernon (also designed by Ariss). Most of the large Virginia plantation houses had rooms for dancing, but some of the most notable survivors are at Sabine Hall (not open to the public), where large balls were held in the upstairs hall, and the Lee family's Stratford Hall, now believed to have been one of Peter Harrison's first designs (ca.1738). Reflecting the emphasis on cotillions rather than longways dances later in the century, the ballrooms at Battersea in Petersburg (possibly by Harrison) and Prestwould, the Skipwith mansion near the North Carolina border, are nearly square in shape.

The principal city of North Carolina, Wilmington, was insignificant compared to most of the cities in the other colonies, but a fine courthouse/market was built there to Harrison's designs about 1740, and assemblies were held upstairs; the building no longer stands. The large upstairs room at the 1767 courthouse at Edenton, designed by John Hawks, was often used for dances, and many fine balls were held at the Tryon Palace (governor's mansion) at New Bern, also designed by Hawks in the late 1760s.

South Carolina was once a hotbed of country dance, even if it no longer is today. One of Peter Harrison's first designs was for Drayton Hall near Charleston, 1738, and its upstairs ballroom is one of the finest in America; it is open to the public through the Natrional Trust. The Exchange or Customhouse, built on the Charleston waterfront in the late 1760s to designs by the Irish architect, William Rigby Naylor, has a large ballroom, where George Washington was entertained after his inauguration as President. Hampton Plantation was enlarged late in the century to include a two-storey ballroom.

Few buildings survive from the eighteenth century in Georgia, thanks to the ravages of fire, weather and wars, but the residents of Savannah are known to have carried on an active program of dances.

The Spanish are known to have adopted country dancing, just as did the rest of Europe, but Florida was of so little importance that there were probably few dances there, whereas there were many balls at Havana, Cuba, where large areas of the eighteenth-century sector of the city have been impressively restored, including some private ballrooms. The only surviving rooms for dancing in French and Spanish Louisiana can be found at some of the oldest plantation houses, a few of which were designed by the former slave, architect Charles Paquet.

Most of the houses in Bermuda were small because it was not a wealthy colony, but Peter Harrison appears to have designed one large house there, Orange Grove (not open to the public), and no doubt balls were held there.

Balls were held in plantation great houses all over the Caribbean, and presumably also at statehouses and courthouses, just as in the mainland British colonies. These statehouses would include those designed by Peter Harrison in Spanish Town, Jamaica; Basseterre, Saint Kitts; Saint John's, Antigua; and Bridgetown, Barbados, and Harrison's governors mansions at Nassau, Bahamas (no longer standing) and Spanish Town, Jamaica; the latter, known as the King's House, burned down many years ago, but its handsome front wall still stands, and two pictures survive of the ballroom there.

How were dances done in the colonial period, compared to the way they are done today? Experts disagree considerably, and the evidence is at least a little ambiguous. Without a videotape made 200 or so years ago, we will never know for sure, but we can study pictures made by good artists and read letters, diaries and books, and can form some conclusions.

Some experts say that in the late colonial period, all dances were danced as triple-minors so as to give every third couple a chance to chat or flirt while they were doing little or nothing for that round of the dance. Perhaps some groups did that, but three of the only four pictures of longways dances from the second half of the eighteenth century clearly show all couples dancing at the same time and no threes waiting out, so the conclusion is that it was not a wide-spread practice.

Some experts also say that 200 or more years ago a dance started with only the top couple in the set active, and everyone else became active only after they had danced with that top couple, in much the same way as Scottish dances are done today. Again, perhaps some groups followed that procedure, which is particularly helpful when the top couple is the only one on the floor that knows the dance, but the famous engraving by Hogarth from the mid-1750s shows that everyone was active at once; the way we know that is that the future King George III is clearly shown at the head of the set, where he would have been placed as a matter of course for each dance, and yet all the dancers were active before he reached them. The conclusion is that having only the top couple active was not very wide-spread.

A third area in dispute among experts concerns exotic French steps. Did English and American dancers use them, or did they generally use the same simple steps used by modern country dancers, such as the walking, skipping, slipping (chasser) and skip-change steps? Dance masters, who needed to make country dance sound as complicated as possible to make sure they could count on a long-term job, definitely tried to teach minuet and bourree and other exotic steps, but, human nature being what it is, most dancers are likely to have rejected the complicated steps. How do we know that? First of all, the surviving pictures do not show any. In the case of Hogarth and Rowlandson, both hated things French, so if the dancers they were depicting were doing anything obviously French these artists would certainly have exaggerated it in their pictures. Hogarth, in fact, did do a portrait of French-trained dance-master, John Essex, and managed to make him appear slimy and effete just standing still, so he had the ability to bring out those characteristics if he saw them.

Furthermore, thanks to research by Kate Keller, we know that very few dance masters in America had French surnames, except in a very short period from 1792 to 1802, which represents the period in which many people had to flee from the excesses of the French Revolution, until they felt safe returning to the stability offered by Napoleon. This period corresponds to a flood of letters and diary entries of dancers complaining that dancing was no longer as much fun as it used to be because of the difficult steps that dancers were being forced to learn. This suggests that exotic steps had previously been the exception rather than the rule.

Some experts suggest that exotic steps, therefore, were a function of the occasion. For example, they may have been essential at a ball at the Williamsburg Governor's Palace but less so at an assembly in the Apollo Room at the Raleigh Tavern. Since many of the same people would have attended both events, such a conclusion does not seem warranted. In the first place, if the dancers at Wanstead House, one of the great houses of England (now destroyed), with the future George III present were clearly not using exotic steps, there is no reason to suppose that dancers in the Governor's Palace would. The best answer is that a few dancers used exotic steps wherever they danced, but the total number of such dancers in both England and America can not have been anything but small.

My personal conclusion is that average dancers two or three centuries ago danced remarkably similarly to the way we dance today, making allowances for the restrictions imposed by some of the clothing of the day (some period stayles, for example, prevented the wearer from raising the elbows even as high as the shoulders, and nearly all people were forced into a particular way of carrying the upper body erect), with the exception of a few figures here and there that were misinterpreted by Cecil Sharp and his followers over the years.

Costumed country dance balls and assemblies are held regularly in many communities today, many of them sponsored by affiliates of the Country Dance & Song Society. The following list is by no means complete, but it will serve to illustrate that the tradition is alive and well, and perhaps growing every year.: Peterborough, Ontario; Brattleboro, Vermont; Boston, Massachusetts; Newport, Rhode Island (where the 1752 Turtle Frolic is re-enacted every 23rd December at the Sheraton Hotel on Goat Island); Hartford, Connecticut; New York City; Princeton, New Jersey; Philadelphia, Pennsylvania; Dover, Delaware; Baltimore, Frederick and Saint Mary's City, Maryland; Williamsburg, Richmond, Louisa and Alexandria, Virginia; Nashville, Tennessee; and Bath, England.

A word of caution: English country dancers are used to a particular title referring to a specific set of dance instructions and a specific tune. Such was probably the norm for any group of dancers in the eighteenth century as well, but it was not necessarily the norm on a worldwide basis. Many examples exist of a given title referring to two or more completely different dance tunes, and in some cases over a dozen different sets of dance instructions. For the sake of producing this book, the author has subjectively chosen the tune or set of instructions that most appealed to him in such cases where he was aware of more than one in either category, unless one of them had some compelling historical reason for being more important than the others. In some cases, such as Jamaica and Lilli Burlero, the dance instructions published in two places differ from each other simply because of a mistake in one of the editions. Even though this may cause pain to those who have enjoyed dancing those two dances to the familiar instructions (as inrterpreted by Cecil Sharp), other early dance publications show that these dances suffered from serious typographical errors in Playford, so these dances are shown in this book in corrected form.

Here are the criteria for including dances in this book: first, America means Canada, the United States, Bermuda and British and French Caribbean islands. Dances in English and European books with names referring to America or things American; dances in English or European books that are known to have been owned by people living in America; dances mentioned in historical American accounts; dances found in early American manuscripts or published books; dances whose tunes are found in early American manuscripts.

11

In the eighteenth century, many dance assemblies were strictly regulated according to published rules. Two sets of such rules are given here, the first from Newport, RI in 1747, and the second from Savannah, GA in 1789.

Rules for the Regulation of the Assembly Commenced Octbr 28th: 1747 in Newport.

1st: Every member at the time of Subscription shall pay the Steward Four Pounds, To defray the Charges of the First and Second Evenings.

2nd: That on the first Night of our Meeting as well as at other times, Every Member shall pay Fourty Shillings to the Steward, that he may always have a Sufficient Stock on advance to defray the Expence of the two Subsequent Evenings.

3rd: That a Steward or Master of the Ceremony shall be chosen from Among the Subscribers, who shall Continue in office A Fortnight or two Evenings, At the Expiration of which time he shall appoint another of the Subscribers to Succeed him ToWhom he shall give an exact account of the Money Received and disbursed; in a regular book to be open to the Inspection of all the Members, And in which shall be a Copy of these Rules and orders to be kept for that purpose.

4th: The Steward shall be obliged to Nominate a person to succeed him who has not been before Appointed; that each Gentleman may discharge the office in his turn, after which there shall be a Constant and regular Succession as they were at first Appointed.

5th: No Member if he bee in Town and in Health shall be absent from the Assembly on the penalty of three Pounds To be paid to the Steward who shall be Accomptable.

6th: If any member shall upon his Word of Honour declare that to his certain knowledge any Absent Member was in Other Company of an Assembly Evening, So as to Neglect coming (unless upon some Spesciall Occasion, his being with Strangers not to be Allowed a Sufficient Excuse.) Such Absent Member shall then not be excused his Fine, Or if he is tardy, he shall be fined at the discretion of the Steward, Who shall give him Notice of it.

7th: That the Steward shall be particularly careful that the expence of one Night do not exceed the money Subscribed, Which if he do so shall be at his own loss, but if the expence do not ballance the Subscription he shall be Accomptable To his Successor for the Money not Expended.

8th: At such times as the Fines and advanced Money shall be sufficient for defraying the Expences of the next Evening (Exclusive of the Advanced Subscription) the Members shall be Excused from paying any thing.

9th: The Steward shall provide a proper Person to deal out the Tea, Coffee, Wine etc: Prepared for the Accommodation of the Company.

10th: Any member Gentleman or Lady shall be at liberty to introduce any Stranger whom they shall Judge proper and Agreable To the Company.

11th: Every member at the time of Subscribing shall be presented with a list of Such Ladies, as are to have a general Invitation To each of whom will be given a Ticket for their Constant Admittance.

12th: The Assembly shall begin at Six in the Evening and break up at Twelve, and no Member shall take its amiss of the Master of the Ceremonies when he insists upon it.

13th: No new member to be Admitted but such as shall be approved off by the Majority of the Subscribers Present at the Assembly when he shall be proposed, (the Steward to have the Casting Vote.)

14th: For the sake of keeping up the decorum and Regularity of this Assembly, if any member uses or takes any Indecent Liberty or Familiarity with any of the Ladies, Such Member shall pay Five Pounds for the first Offence, and for the Second shall be, by the Steward Publicly Expelled the Assembly.

15th: If any Married Gentleman has an Inclination of coming to the Assembly with his Lady, Such Gentleman shall be Admitted (but not to Subscribe) upon the same footing as any of the other members, i.e. (Paying an Equal Proportion of the Expence of the Evening.)

16th: With respect to Dancing of Minuets, the Gentlemen shall dance with such Ladies As the Master of the Ceremonies shall Appoint And of Sett or Cuntrey dances, the usual Method of drawing numbers Shall be Observed (the first Numbers to have thePrecedency) with this priviledge to the master of the Ceremonies that he shall always chuse his own Partner and open the Ball.

There follows a list of 32 women and only 13 men involved in the Assembly.

The Savannah Assembly's rules were fewer and shorter.

Rules & Regulations for the Dancing Assembly of 1789.

1. The assemblies to commence on the third Wednesday night in December Instant, and to continue once every fortnight throughout the Season.

2. Each assembly to open with minuets, beginning precisely at half past six o'clock.

3. In country dances, the Governor's lady shall be entitled to the first Number without drawing.

4. All other Ladies shall stand agreable to the Number which they draw, Brides and Strangers excepted, who, for one Evening, shall be entitled to the second Number without drawing.

5. No Lady shall call more than one Dance, and the Figure which she sets shall be observed through the whole without variation unless altered with her consent; and no Lady shall dance out of her set but by permission of the managers.

6. Every Lady shall stand up when her number is called, and no Lady shall sit down till every couple shall have gone through the dance.

7. Every Lady and Gentleman shall have the privilege of engaging their own partners; but if there should be any Lady unengaged or any Gentleman not a subscriber, the manager will endeavor to engage partners for them.

8. No Gentleman residing in, or within 15 miles of, the town, who is not a subscriber shall be admitted.

9. Strangers to be admitted by aprobation of the managers, on their paying two dollars a ticket.

10. Any subscriber Introducing a Stranger (Lady or Gentleman) shall be answerable for any improper Introduction.

11. No card playing till the country dances begin. No Gentleman to be admitted in boots.

12. There shall be six managers chosen, two of whom shall officiate each night, who shall have full power to regulate and conduct the entertainment, as they think proper. No acting manager to dance for the night.

13. There shall be a treasurer appointed, who shall receive and account for all monies to the manager.

Set of English delftware tiles ca.1700 showing dancers in a square dance, several years after the last publication of directions for such a dance—the earliest known picture of a square dance. The dance is most likely "Newcastle," in the phrase, Forward a double and back. Note the fontanges or high headpieces on the two women at left, typical of the period.

DANCE STEPS AND FIGURES

As mentioned above, a certain amount of controversy exists, which will probably not be resolved any time soon, concerning the kind of steps appropriate for country dances. In many cases, the steps used depended upon the rhythm of the music. All country dance steps can be divided into travelling and setting (non-travelling) steps. The travelling steps are covered first.

The most common rhythm is the march, reel or hornpipe, in which each bar contains two beats (written 2/2 or 2/4), each of which may be divided (for musical purposes but not dance purposes) into a further two or four beats. The jig (written 6/8) also has two beats to the bar, but each of its beats can be divided musically into triplets or three notes. Appropriate travelling steps for these rhythms are the walk; the skip (step right, hop right, step left, hop left, etc.); the skip-change (starting with a hop on the left foot BEFORE the first beat of the phrase, step right, close with left, step right, hop right, step left, close with right, step left, hop left, etc.); a modified double step (right, left, right, hop right, left, right, left, hop left, etc.); and the bourrée-4 (with heels off the floor, right, left, right, pause sinking with left heel touching right ankle; left, right, left, pause sinking with right heel touching left ankle, etc.). Much of Elizabethan dance was in double or single steps (one double equals right, left, right and close; a single equals a step with either foot and close); one eighteenth-century French step occasionally used (sometimes as a result of the instructions, sometimes by personal whim) in place of the double step is the contretemps (with left toe pointed forward and down a few inches off the floor, hop on the right, step left, step right, close with left; only occasionally done starting on the other foot). Directions that include the contretemps are often confusing, as they will say "2 contretemps" when they merely mean "a double step using a contretemps."

In seventeenth-century Scotland, musicians developed a way of playing reels (and occasionally other rhythms at an early date) in slow tempo that became known as strathspey. The earliest records of dances done to strathspey time found thus far come from shortly after the middle of the eighteenth century. Without the videotapes we so much need for so many aspects of historical life no solid evidence exists as to the travelling step used in the strathspey, but it seems logical to assume that a slow version of the skip-change would be correct, similar to the modern strathspey step (which is apparently also similar to a complicated French step called the contretemps de gavotte). About half the period pictures of strathspeys show the men with their hands above their heads and upper arms parallel with the floor, so this would be appropriate for historical dancing, but would be close to scandalous to modern Scottish country dancers.

Another frequently-used duple-time step is the chasser or slip step, in which the dancer moves sideways and the trailing foot never quite catches up to the leading foot. This is best done with heels off the floor. The chasser is usually done for 4 or 8 steps at a time, and on the last count the dancer ends with feet together, ready to move off again in whatever direction is required. In the interest of standardization, when dancers are directed to slip a circle in both directions, always start to the left first (clockwise), although a few eighteenth-century dance books called for going to the right first, which merely means that things were not as well standardized in those days before the telephone, television and jet aircraft as perhaps they ought to have been.

Among the duple-time rhythms is the strathspey. Theoretically, since a strathspey tune is supposed to be a reel played at slow speed its time signature could be 2/2 or 2/4, but since at slow speed the danceable beats are four to a measure the proper way to write a strathspey is actually 4/4. This rule is probably disobeyed as often as it is obeyed, so expect to find strathspeys written either in 2 or in 4.

The bourrée-4 and the contretemps are the only exotic French steps used in duple-time dances, and it is important to understand their limitations. First of all, probably only a small percentage of English and American dancers ever used them at all before 1792. Second, they were not used all the way through a dance, but only in certain figures. The reason for this is simple: these steps do not cover as much ground as the walking or skip-change steps, so when you need to cover ground fast do not use exotic steps. On the other hand, some figures allow plenty of time to get around, time that is often filled by expanding the size of the loops, and these figures—such as ordinary rights & lefts—can be appropriately danced in these exotic steps. It would not be appropriate to use them, for example, in down the middle, back & cast off, because timing is so critical in order that you not inconvenience other dancers.

Dances in triple time have (time signature: 3/2 or 3/4 or slipjig 9/8) a greater variety of exotic steps available, which however does not mean that such steps were widely used. One step that was NOT used is the modern waltz step (even in a dance with the word waltz in the title, such as the Duke of Kent's Waltz) with its long-short-short pattern. The simplest way to dance in triple time is to take even walking steps throughout.

The bourree-3 was designed to be used with triple-time music, and it is danced with heels off the floor. Starting just before the first beat of the measure, sink, but rise up again on the first beat. Right, left, right and sink, left, right, left and sink, etc. The beats are, of course, all even, and it takes a certain amount of coordination to squeeze the sink and rise into the space between bars.

The most famous of the triple-time steps is the minuet, and the directions for a few country dances specifically call for the minuet step, which can be daunting at first. One thing to remember is that there was no one minuet step but a great variety of them, and my strong suspicion is (without a period videotape I am afraid it can not be proved either way) that the word minuet referred more to the tempo than the actual step. In other words, some dancers, with perhaps less coordination or energy than others, felt quite comfortable in dancing the minuet or minuet-country-dances with either a bourrée-3 or a walking step, and that such steps were acceptable minuet steps; the minuet step could be anything you wanted it to be as long as you were clearly following some pattern, no matter how simple.

In spite of the foregoing, clearly a few English and American dancers were quite accomplished with a more complicated minuet step. The most basic one can be thought of as a single followed by a double, and is, of course, danced with heels off the floor. When feet are together at the end of each single and the end of each double, sink briefly; the best dancers manage to keep the trailing foot just off the floor during the sink. Thus, even though the music is three beats to the bar, the minuet step takes six beats or two bars, and no one ever managed to re-order the writing of the music to match the dancing.

In conclusion, the minuet steps were what kept the dance masters employed, so if you have the inclination, the time and the coordination, by all means feel free to learn one or other of the complicated steps, but if you have not some of these attributes you will not be wrong in dancing with the bourrée-3 or walking steps, but bear one thing in mind: the complicated minuet steps do not cover much ground for all their time and effort, so the simpler steps should be taken in small size to avoid covering ground too quickly if others are using the complicated steps.

The non-travelling or setting step for duple-time tunes has a wide variety of possibilities. In the sixteenth century, setting was merely a single step to one side and then a single back to the other—step to the right and close, step to the left and close. After a while, it became obvious that the setting step was an occasion for showing off individuality without interfering with any other dancer. Late in the sixteenth century, one such step was codified in the directions of the dance "Althea," and some dancers will recognize it as the modern kick-balance, beloved of contradancers: step on the right foot and kick to the right with the left foot with toe down (be careful not to kick other dancers; they don't like it), then step on the left foot and kick the right foot to the left.

The French invented the balancer, a graceful version of the original setting step: with heels off the ground, step to the right, keeping the left toe where it was until the last possible moment, then bring the left heel in to touch the right ankle and sink the right heel to the floor; repeat in the other direction —very elegant when properly executed.

Another French invention is the rigadoon (English for pas de rigaudon). In years past, it has been fashionable to do the rigadoon as follows: point the right toe straight out to the right; pull the right foot back to place while the left toe points out to the left; pull the left foot back to place; hop in place (or, as some people do it, jump up in the air with legs apart and bring them back together the moment before landing). Recent research suggests that this is not entirely correct, and a new interpretation (by no means the only one) is thus: flick the right toe out to the side and pull it back instantly; flick the left toe out to the side and pull it back instantly; plier (bend the knees); straighten up again, with or without a little hop. Whichever way you do it, it takes four counts (two bars), like all duple-time setting steps.

Another setting step occasionally seen is the Beaten step: point the right toe out to the right; with toe pointed down, bring the right foot behind the left calf; point the right toe out again to the right; bring the right foot back to place. This works particularly well where the instruction is to set twice, and then you can do a Beaten step to the right, followed by one to the left; another way to put variety into setting twice is to do balancer followed by rigadoon.

When Cecil Sharp revived historical country dance early this century, he concluded that the setting step should be bouncier than a simple single to each side, so the standard setting step among modern country dancers is: step to the right; bring the left foot over and change weight to it for just an instant before putting weight back onto the right; then repeat in the other direction. Dr. Jean Milligan's revival of Scottish country dance came up with a variation on that theme, the pas de Basque (too complicated to explain here; ask one of your Scottish dancing friends to demonstrate it), in which the heels rise higher off the ground than Sharp's step, followed by a jeter by the trailing foot. This is entirely appropriate for historical dancing, as far as can be determined. The strathspey (four beats to the measure) refers to the slow tempo of playing known in parts of Scotland for many years, but the earliest references of dancing to that tempo appear to date no further back than the 1760s. Nevertheless, the strathspey setting step was described (under a different name, but in two Scottish dances) in the French book, Orchesographie in 1589. The step is essentially a double step to the right followed by a double step to the left: with heels off the ground, step to the right, close, step to the right again, close with a hop and with left foot behind right calf, toe pointing down; then repeat in the other direction.

The setting step in triple time has to be a slow balancer—nothing else will really fit with any grace. Balance to the right in three counts and balance to the left in three counts.

Country Dances are directional. It is necessary to establish in which direction the "presence" is located, a term that once referred to where royalty would be seated to watch the dancing, or, failing that, usually where the musicians were situated; that direction is called "up" or "above," while the other direction is obviously "down" or "below." In longways dances, the men find the presence to their left, and the women find it to their right; when men and women are on their correct side, they are called "proper," and when they are crossed over to the opposite side they are called "improper." In a cotillion, the head couples are those with their backs or faces to the presence, and the others are called side couples.

In a longways dance, dancers encounter other dancers by means of the progression. This takes place each time the tune is played through completely, and, if the tune is repeated enough times, the progression gives all the couples an opportunity to take on the "active" role of the number one couples. At the end of each round of the dance, the ones will have progressed one place down the set, while the twos progress one place up the set (in a triple-minor set, the twos become threes as well as moving up, while the threes become twos for the next round of the dance but do not progress up the set until they have danced as twos). When ones reach the bottom or twos reach the top of a duple set, they wait out one round and then rejoin the dance as the opposite number from what they had before. In a triple-minor dance, the progression is slightly more complicated, for, although the ones remain ones all the way to the bottom, the other dancers switch back and forth between being twos and threes until they reach the top, at which point they have to wait out more than one round before they can come in as ones. In addition, ones approaching the bottom will find that they will have to dance one round with imaginary threes in order to reach the foot.

Cotillions are entirely different. They were adapted by the French from Elizabethan English square dances. They have no progression, but are divided into a series of standard verses (called changes) each followed by a chorus (known as the figure) peculiar to that particular cotillion. Normally, three or four changes are selected by the Dance master from a pool of changes known to all the dancers, except that the Grand Round is always the first change.

The progression

Duple-Minor Longways

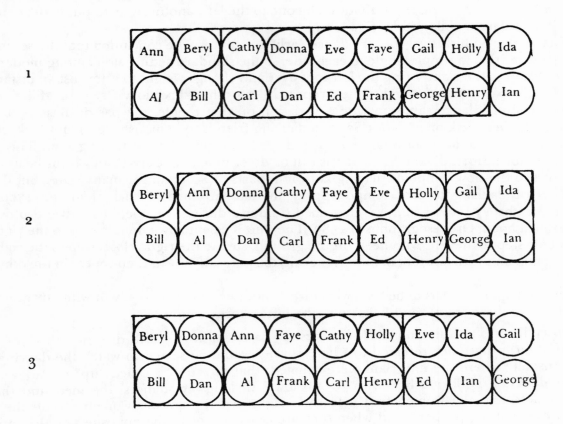

A few points of terminology and style remain to be covered before the dance figures are examined. The identification of one's partner is obvious, but certain other people are called opposites, corners, contraries and neighbours. In a cotillion, a man's corner is usually the women to his left, while a woman's corner is usually the man to her right. In a longways set, 1 Man and 2 Woman are First Corners, and 2 Man and 1 Woman are Second Corners. In a cotillion, one's opposite is the person of the opposite sex directly across the set. In a triple-minor longways set, the person in number two position (usually the number one person who has already progressed) looks across the set diagonally to the right to see the first contrary and across the set diagonally to the left to see the second contrary (contrary is short for contrary corner). One's neighbour is the person next along the line *within the minor set*.

Country Dancing depends to a certain extent on proper use of hands and arms. When dancers take hands for a turn or a star, they should use a normal hand-shake grip, and not any special wrist or thumb grip invented in more recent times. The hands should be slightly below the elbows, which in turn should be below the shoulders; the arms should form a catenary curve under tension from the shoulder of one dancer to the shoulder of the other (the cut of many women's gowns prevented them from raising their arms higher). In a turn or star, each dancer should lean slightly outwards to keep the tension, but when slipping around in a ring, strangely enough, the dancers should lean slightly forward (inward) to maintain the correct tension and keep the circle round.

All Country Dances should begin and end with Honours to one's partner. Many musical groups, both live and recorded, neglect to give the important music at the beginning for bows and courtesies (curtsy is a contraction for courtesy), a practice that is to be deplored. Various ways of honour-

Triple-minor longways

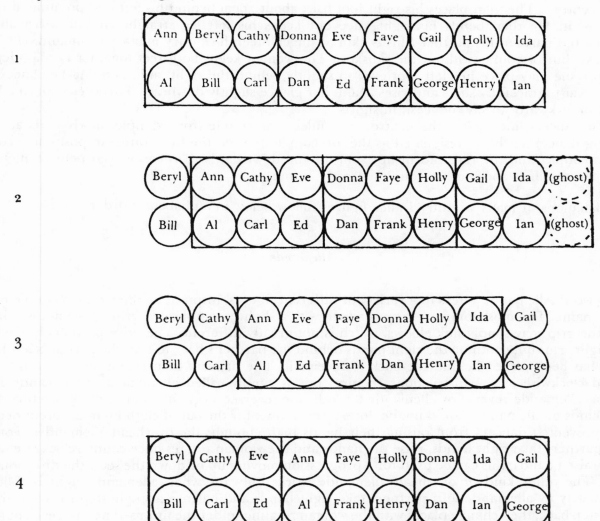

1

| Ann | Beryl | Cathy | Donna | Eve | Faye | Gail | Holly | Ida |
| Al | Bill | Carl | Dan | Ed | Frank | George | Henry | Ian |

2

| Beryl | Ann | Cathy | Eve | Donna | Faye | Holly | Gail | Ida | (ghost) |
| Bill | Al | Carl | Ed | Dan | Frank | Henry | George | Ian | (ghost) |

3

| Beryl | Cathy | Ann | Eve | Faye | Donna | Holly | Ida | Gail |
| Bill | Carl | Al | Ed | Frank | Dan | Henry | Ian | George |

4

| Beryl | Cathy | Eve | Ann | Faye | Holly | Donna | Ida | Gail |
| Bill | Carl | Ed | Al | Frank | Henry | Dan | Ian | George |

Cotillions

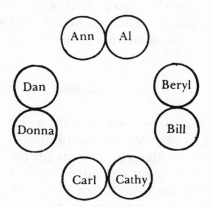

19

ing have been used over the years, but one particular way seems to have been popular in the eighteenth century. The man places his right foot back about 30cm behind his left and pointing at right angles to it. He then bends his right knee but keeps his left leg straight and his waist almost straight, and gazes at his partner (this is akin to the eighteenth-century military command, "Present firelocks!" but of course without the musket.) The women keeps both feet together at a 45-degree angle, or she may place her left foot ever so slightly behind the right, and, bending her knees but not her waist, gracefully sinks and rises again, her glance slightly downcast. This is elegant in a long gown but awkward, to say the least, in shorts!

When dancers line up for the next dance, unless one couple (for example, newly-weds at their wedding dance) has been designated as the top couple in a set, the first couple in position becomes the top couple, and the ranks form up from the top downwards. It is considered poor etiquette to try to join the lines above other couples already in line.

Explanations of many Country Dance figures follow below in alphabetical order.

Allemande

The word Allemande refers to a variety of different figures, inspired by the German couple-dance of that name. The most common form is a turn with a slightly complicated grip; those not wishing to learn the grip may simply link elbows, which is not greatly different. The grip: partners link elbows with right arms but continue the right hands behind the partner's back to grip the partner's left hand, which has been placed behind the back to receive it. The dancers then rotate once or 1 1/2 times around clockwise as the instructions require; this is simply called allemande or allemande right, whereas allemande reverse or allemande left calls for reversed grip and counterclockwise turn. Two other kinds of allemandes could not be done by everyone, for the cut of clothing in different decades often prevented dancers from raising their hands high enough: the overhead allemandes. For one kind, partners take right hands, raise the hands and the woman rotates once counterclockwise under the upraised hands; this can be used for a progression moving up or down the set if the directions call for it. The other kind of overhead allemande works only for when allemande right is followed immediately by allemande left: partners take right hands and balance a single step forward, then a single step back, then change places with the woman rotating under the upraised hands; reach out with the left hands and repeat with left hands back to places.

Back to Back

In this figure, which is also called Dos-à-dos or do-si-do, two dancers face each other, move forwards and pass each other by right shoulders; then, each one moves slightly to his right and dances backwards back to the original place, having passed the other dancer by left shoulders on the way back. Dancers continue facing in the same direction throughout the figure—no turns or flips.

Casting

Casting is a movement that begins by turning to face the direction opposite to that in which one wishes to go before continuing to turn to face the desired direction. For example, in the most commonly-found situation, a man in a longways set casts off (ie., down) into second place by turning to his left to face up, then out, then down. When he arrives in second place, he will have traced a spiral on the floor. In casting up, he would turn to face down first. In a longways set, every time the 1s cast off, the 2s should move up into the 1s' place, usually on beats 5, 6, 7 and 8. To lead a cast, the 1s cast down (or up), followed by the 2s and 3s to invert the set.

Change Places or Cross

Two dancers change places by passing by right shoulders unless otherwise directed. Passing by right shoulders is probably derived from the English custom of passing by right shoulders on foot or on horseback (and now in motorcars) so that sword hilts (worn on the left) would not lock. When corners cross, unless directions say otherwise, First Corners (people in 1 Man and 2 Woman places) change first.

Circle

Dancers take hands in a ring, their arms in a catenary curve, and dance around the ring clockwise unless otherwise directed. The normal step for this is the walking step, but on many occasions the slipping step is more appropriate (in which case one lands on feet-together on count 8).

Cloverleaf—see Turn Single
Dos-à-Dos—see Back to Back

A Double

A double step—a term going back at least to the fifteenth century—refers actually to four steps, in which one travels for three steps and brings feet together on the fourth count. Frequently, the instructions call for forward a double and back, which means to go forward a double step, starting on the right foot (sometimes with very small steps to avoid colliding with other dancers), and when that is completed to go ("fall") backwards a double step.

Down the Middle and Back

This figure, which appears in the majority of longways dances, is one of the few opportunities for dancers to show individuality without unduly upsetting the other dancers. The basic figure is as follows: the 1s take near hands and, with a walking step, dance down the middle for six counts, turn around individually, come back up the middle and cast off into second place, the 2s moving up on the last four counts (figure totals 16 counts). Some dances specifically call for dancing down the middle, back and no cast-off, since the progression comes at another point, and others call for down the middle and back to progressed places without a cast-off (ie., the 2s move up out of the way before the 1s come back up that far), in which case the 1s ought to dance down for at least 8 counts. Some of the alternatives to the first (walking) figure that need no special instructions: A) use a skip-change step instead of a walking step; B) 1s dance with a walking step down the middle for 8 counts (best with right hand to right hand so as to give partner a clue to what you are planning), turn, skip back and cast off; C) 1s take both hands, chasser down the middle for 4 counts, rigadoon, chasser back and cast off; D) 1s take near hands and dance with walking step down the middle for 4 counts, take two hands and turn once around clockwise in 4 counts, dance back up and cast off; E) 1s dance down the middle with walking step and turn as a couple (man backing up), come back up improper and the man hands the woman across in front of him to get proper again. Be inventive; our forefathers were.

Figure-8 and Half Figure-8

In a figure-8, a dancer traces a figure-8 over the floor by weaving a path around two other stationary dancers. When two dancers do a figure-8 around the same other couple, the dancing couple cross, the man allowing the woman to go in front of him each time they meet; the man goes first around the stationary woman and the woman around the stationary man; then the man goes around the man and the woman goes around the woman until both dancers are back to original places. For a half figure 8, only the first half of the figure-8 is done, leaving the dancers on the opposite side from where they started. In a triple-minor set, a figure-8 is sometimes done by the 1s from middle (progressed) places, one dancer doing the figure around the twos while the other does it around the threes.

Gate

Neighbours take near hands and rotate so that the dancer below comes forwards up the middle of the set and down the outside, while the dancer above backs around the same pathway until they end in the same places where they began.

Hands Across—see Star

Hey

Heys abound in great variety, but they are essentially weaving figures in which everyone moves, unlike the figure-8 in which the weaving is done around a stationary couple. For a circular hey, see under *Rights and Lefts*. In a longways triple-minor set, three kinds of linear heys are found. In the Mirror Hey, the 1s face down while the 2s dance out and up ("middles bulge"), and the 3s come together to take hands briefly. Then the 1s dance out and down to the bottom while the 3s dance up the middle and the 2s come together at the top to take hands briefly. Each couple follows the same figure-8 track-way until all are back in original places (16 counts).

In a Crossover Hey, the 2s and 3s dance as if doing a regular mirror hey, but the 1s start by crossing over as they head down the set (the woman going in front of the man) and go out between the 2s and 3s on the improper sides and complete the hey on the improper sides. Often (but not always) the 1s will then cross back to the proper sides while all three couples execute a second crossover hey.

Heys at Top and bottom are danced across the set. The 1s start in second (progressed) place, and one of them goes up between the 2s to start a hey with them and the other goes down between the 3s to start a hey with them. The 1 Man always starts the hey by going around the woman of the other couple first, and the 1 Woman goes around the man. They follow the regular figure-8 pathway until the heys are complete and the 1s return to progressed places.

Ladies Chain

In the eighteenth century, this figure was apparently confined to cotillions, although in the nineteenth century it became a popular figure in longways dances as well. Opposite women take right hands and pull past, and then give left hands to the opposite man and turn by the left once around into the opposite woman's place (8 counts); the modern invention of the man assisting the woman with his right hand behind her back (called a courtesy turn) is historically incorrect.

Lead a Cast—see Cast

Pattacake

Partners face, clap own hands, then clap partner's right hand to right, then clap own hands, then clap partner's left hand to left hand.

Poussette

Partners take both hands. The upper man pushes his partner towards the wall on the women's side while the lower man pulls his partner towards the men's wall until the couples are clear of each other. At this point the upper couple manoeuvres slightly down the set (while still facing in the same direction) while the other couple moves up the set, and they push or pull back into lines in progressed places, thus far, the figure is a half poussette. A whole poussette is simply the continuation of the process back to original places, a total of 16 counts. A poussette is, in effect, for couples what back-to-back is for individuals. It is nearly always clockwise (the word comes from the French *pousser*, to push, and the instruction is intended for the man in the first position), but by the nineteenth century some books called it "draw," suggesting counter-clockwise rotation—one of many mistakes or alterations that crept into dancing after 1800.

Rights and Lefts

A weaving figure in which dancers pass by taking hands, first right hands and then left. If the weaving is done without hands, it is called a circular hey. If more than two couples at a time are involved in the same chain it can be called a grand chain. Normally, partners face to start rights and lefts, and the figure is confined to the first and second couples in the minor set. Four changes return the dancers to original places, whereas three changes make a progression. Some dances manage to use just two changes. Be sure to continue turning the same way—the shortest way—as you go around the little circle of four dancers.

Setting

In its most common form, setting is no more than a step to the right and close followed by a step to the left and close, taking four beats. Very often, setting is done by partners to each other, which means that one zigs while the other zags (if they are both moving to their own right, they are going in opposite directions), and that partners should take advantage of this opportunity to interact with each other by setting not exactly to the side but slightly forwards towards each other.

The setting step has traditionally afforded dancers the greatest opportunity for individual expression; we read about sailors, for example, who would spend off-watch hours "footing it" or setting to partners on the foredeck of their ship, presumably trying to invent ever more impressive variations. Among the variations more often used are the Scottish Pas de Basque; a simplified Pas de Basque without the kick at the end of each half; the Rigadoon (see above); the Beaton step; and the modern contradancers' kick—balance (actually invented in the sixteenth century!). These variations are better demonstrated in person by someone who knows them rather than explained in a book.

Siding

Siding is an Elizabethan figure that still occasionally appeared in eighteenth-century dances. Partners advance a double step (with small actual steps) to end with right shoulder next to right shoulder, then fall back a double to places; this is normally repeated, left shoulder to left shoulder, but sometimes with another figure in between. Cecil Sharp invented a siding figure in 1911 when his research failed to show him the historical figure, and the Sharp siding is often used by modern country dancers; although it is graceful, it has no place in any historical dances.

Star

The star, or "hands across" as is it called in historical dance books, is usually danced by four people. Dancers reach into the middle with right hands and take the hand of the dancer diagonally across from them in a handshake grip; the hands should be below the shoulders and the arms should be under slight tension. The dancers then move the star around clockwise back to places, or occasionally only half way around. A right-hand star is often followed by a left-hand star, which rotates counterclockwise. No fancy thumb or wrist grips should be used in historical dances.

Turn

As in a star, two dancers take right hands as if to shake hands, making sure that the hands are below the shoulders and that the arms are under reasonable tension. They turn eachother once around clockwise back to places. Sometimes, a turn can be required to be half, three-quarters, once-and-a-quarter or once-and-a-half around. The same instructions apply to a left-hand turn, except that the dancers rotate counterclockwise. In a two-hand turn, which is always clockwise, the man's hands support the woman's hands.

Turn Single

In spite of its name, the turn single involves a "double step." The word *single* merely instructs the dancer to turn alone. This is not a spin around on one foot, but it is as if one were walking around the rim of an LP record on the floor. It takes four steps, the last one ending with feet together. The turn single is usually to the right or clockwise, but occasionally a turn to the left is indicated; one such occasion is sometimes described as a cloverleaf turn single, in which the dancers in 1 Man and 2 Woman positions turn to the left and the dancers in 2 Man and 1 Woman positions turn to the right. The turn single can also be used as a travelling step for short distances; for example, if it follows, as it often does, setting to partner, the dancers will probably have moved slightly forwards out of their lines, and the turn single can bring them back into their lines.

Cotillions

Cotillions, as was explained above, are square dances with a series of optional verses or "changes" each followed by the specific chorus or "figure" of that cotillion. The Dance Master chooses which of the well-known changes he desires and calls them accordingly, except that all cotillions begin with the Grand Round. It is appropriate that partners hold near hands all the time except when directed otherwise. Here follow ten of the most straight-forward changes.

1. THE GRAND ROUND
Partners take near hands, set and rigadoon, then all take hands and chasse eight counts to the left. Repeat, with the chassé going to the right back to places.

2. WOMEN'S MOULINET (moulinet is French for windmill)
The women set forwards twice, then do a right-hand star for eight counts. Repeat back to places with a left-hand star.

3. MEN'S MOULINET
The same as the Women's Moulinet. If desired, it is possible for the two moulinets to be combined into a single change, in which the women do the first half and end up back in their places, and then the men do the second half of the moulinet.

4. THE GRAND CHAIN
Partners face to begin a grand rights & lefts around the set, except that each time they meet (on the other side and back home) they take two hands and rigadoon. A skipping step is appropriate.

5. LADIES' CHAINS
The head women do a ladies chain across to opposite sides, then the side women do likewise; repeat back to places.

6. GRAND SQUARES
The partners face each other in the side couples; they fall back from each other a double, then turn to face their opposite and come forward a double. Take near hands with the opposite and come a double towards the centre. Then take partner's near hand and fall back a double to places; WHILE the heads take near hands, come forwards a double to the centre, take near hands with opposite, fall back into side positions, face, separate, and fall back a double. Then turn to face partners and come forwards a double to places. Then both heads and sides repeat the figure, going in the reverse directions.

7. WEAVE RINGS (popularly known as "the Grand Leer")
Partners face and the men pass their partners by right shoulders, pass the next woman by left shoulders, the next by right, and so forth back to places. Then the women do likewise, starting by passing partners by left shoulders.

8. NEWCASTLE ARCHES
Head partners take near hands, lead forward a double, change hands and lead out two steps and make an arch. Side people separate, cast off and come in through the arches and all return to places. Then sides do what heads did and vice versa.

9. HYDE PARK IN & OUT
Head partners take both hands and chasse to the middle; drop hands and take both hands with opposite; chasse out the sides, the side partners separating to allow them to pass; heads separate and return to places. Then sides do what heads did.

10. ALLEMANDS
Allemande right with the corner, then allemande left the partner, then allemande right with the corner from the other side of the partner, then allemande left the partner again and end in places.

Pennsylvania-German earthenware dish attributed to Johannes Neis, 1786, showing a scene from 1777–8 during the British occupation of Philadelphia, possibly the Mischianza of 18 May, 1778. The men all wear the red coats of the British military. This is the earliest known picture of country dance in America. The German inscription translates: "Our maid, the ugly pig, who always wanted to be a housewife. Oh, you ugly slut," and it may refer to one of the women in the picture being accused of collaborating with the enemy, or it may have no connection whatsoever with the picture. Philadelphia Museum of Art, Gift of John T. Morris.

PERIOD CLOTHING

Any proper description of period clothing of the seventeenth and eighteenth centuries would undoubtedly extend to a whole book rather than a single chapter, but a brief description ought to help the reader get a feel for the subject before turning to further reading as suggested in our bibliographical references at the end of the chapter.

All women of all social classes wore a simple shift next to their skin, which doubled as a night-gown. It was made of light linen or occasionally cotton. A draw-string around the neck could be adjusted so that the shift could just be seen all around the neck of the bodice; the neck-line was often enhanced by a gathered ruffle or piece of lace, as were the gathered cuffs of the sleeves. The sleeves, incidentally, were designed to come to just below the elbows—women were never supposed to reveal their elbows. The sleeves of the shift were intended to be seen a centimetre or two below the ends of the sleeves of a dress.

Over the shift, women of all social classes wore a petty-skirt. This was a very full skirt that was either gathered or pleated into a waist-band that could be tied or hooked to close it in the back or at the side. Fashionable women wore paniers around the waist under the petty-skirt to make their hips appear wider. Some paniers (French word for basket) were cloth over a metal or bone frame, but the simplest kind was a pair of cloth sacks sewn onto a waist-band, into which one could place the desired amount of stuffing; ideal stuffing today would be used pantyhose.

All women next wore a bodice of one sort or another. Peasant women often wore it as their outermost layer, and for them it was usually not stiffened with any boning. The bodice was laced in the front, and, if the two sides were separated by a gap that would reveal the shift, a loose piece of stiffened cloth called a stomacher was sometimes inserted under the lacing. Middle and upper-class women called the bodice "stays", for in their case it was stiffly boned so as to give their bodies the characteristic shape of the period. If the garment were laced in front it was called a pair of stays, and if laced in the back it was called a corset; needless to say, putting on and taking off a corset requires assistance, whereas stays can be put on and taken off without another person.

A peasant woman required but three other articles of clothing, the most important of which was a hat. The simplest peasant hat was a cap made of a large disk of white muslin drawn small with a draw-string. The outside could be trimmed with a ribbon. For modesty and warmth (the front of the bodice was cut extremely low) a large kerchief or fichu was worn about the shoulders. It could be tucked into the top of the bodice or it could cross over the front and be tied in the back. A fichu was appropriate for all social classes. Finally, a simple muslin apron was worn around the waist, and the top of it was often tucked under the bottom of the bodice.

Some readers may be familiar with the old nursery rhyme, "Lucy Locket lost her pocket." For the most part, pockets were not sewn into women's clothes. However, a separate item of clothing called a pocket could be worn from a cord tied around the waist over the petty skirt. Since pockets were worn to the side it was possible to wear more than one at a time. The pocket was entered through a vertical slit in the top half of its front. The rest of the front was frequently decorated by elaborate embroidery.

Women "of the better sort" usually wore a gown over their bodice and petty-skirt. The gown had its own bodice sewn to a pleated overskirt that was open at the front to reveal the front of the petty-skirt. A typical gown fastened with hooks on the front of the bodice, and many were also adjustable with lacing on the back seam (this lacing was never unfastened, just loosened or tightened to fit the wearer and her condition). The bodices of many gowns were designed so that they did not meet at the top in front by about 10cm and at the bottom by about 4cm, and this gap was filled by a stomacher that was hooked into place; the stomacher was often richly embroidered, or at least made from a contrasting type and color of material from the rest of the gown.

The sleeves ended in a pair of ruffles just below the elbows. The overskirt was pleated before being sewn to the bodice, and was often bunched up in the back by a pair of tapes (no doubt the sailors would have described the tapes as buntlines, which pull up a square sail preparatory to furling it). Each side of the over-skirt would have a slit cut in it for access to a hanging pocket. The gown could be made of heavy or light cloth, and could be a plain colour or a colourful print, a striped (vertical stripes) or a damask. For more formal occasions, a moiré satin was popular or some kind of brocade.

Many women not familiar with stays have a horror of becoming involved with something that is so constraining. Actually, stays need be no more constraining than the wearer wants them to be while they still produce the look required of them. The only time stays need be in the least bit uncomfortable is when you are sitting in the bucket seat of a car or in modern ultra-soft sofas, in which your hips are lower than your knees, and you can probably avoid sitting in such seats while you are wearing stays. I can not stress enough that stays are almost essential for the right period look, for "period" dresses without stays are immediately taken by others as fakes. Since darts (useful for the modern bosom line) were not in vented until after the eighteenth century, the vertical line of the chest was absolutely straight, with the breasts pushed in and up. Stays should be made by an expert, and are not normally something the amateur seamstress should attempt. If you can not obtain stays, you might try stuffing a shaped piece of heavy cardboard inside the front of the bodice.

The gown pattern pieces shown here are, of course, for a gown of a particular date, but a careful seamstress can do necessary research to see how the gowns of other dates differed from this one and make appropriate alterations to the pattern pieces. The basic components were the same from year to year with generally only minor differences that were nonetheless enough to make fashions appear to change drastically.

Nothing need be said about women's shoes, since these were to be hidden under the skirts. However, if it is feared that shoes will be seen, it is probably best to wear simple black dancing slippers or any other "sensible" shoes.

Just as women wore a shift under everything else and also used it as a nightgown, men wore a linen shirt that doubled as a nightshirt. Laborers often wore a colored shirt without ruffles, either in a plain color or in stripes or a check or Madras plaid pattern. Men "of the better sort" wore a white or off-white shirt, and when they wished to dress properly they would add a jabot or cravat around the neck. A jabot was a T-shaped construction, the upright part being covered by a long piece of gathered lace about 6cm deep zig-zagged several times along its front in a cascade. On the shirt itself, the ruffles at the throat opening were usually of plain gathered linen, but they were occasionally lace, as were the ruffles sometimes attached at the cuffs (not shown here). Instead of a jabot, most military men wore a black leather stock that was laced at the back.

The normal attire for the lower half of the body consisted of knee-length stockings (in white silk for those who could afford it) and a pair of breeches. The typical pattern for breeches is, surprisingly, unnecessarily complicated, so a simpler, less common pattern is shown here. The key element is that when the front fall is unbuttoned the breeches will continue to stay on as long as the waistband is fastened. It is important to allow enough room in the seat for bending over or sitting. In some cases, it may be possible to adapt a pair of modern trousers by adding a front fall, cutting off the legs at the calf and tightening around the knee by means of a slit with buttons and a buckled band.

The next item of clothing worn by all men was the waistcoat (what modern Americans call a vest). Historical waistcoats differ from modern vests in a number of ways. First, they had a high neckline, and second, they were much longer. To a certain extent, the earlier the date, the longer the waistcoat and the longer the extent of the row of buttons. Buttons, incidentally, were pewter, brass, wooden, bone, leather or cloth-covered.

The typical coat, except for some (but not all) military coats, was single-breasted. Whereas waistcoats were intended to be completely buttoned (most of the buttons could be left undone for informal moments), after about 1730 or so coats were cut away so that they could not be buttoned, and the buttons were all for show. Most military coats were double-breasted with buttoned-back lapels, and when the weather warranted the left lapel could be brought across and buttoned to the right side buttons. The long skirt of the coat had extra cloth and stiffening made into many folds in order to give it flair. Generally speaking, the earlier the coat, the more extra cloth in the tail.

Clothing for "the better sort" was usually well tailored, and everything was properly lined and hemmed. However, for "the meaner sort," linings were frequently omitted, and the cloth was so tightly woven that it was unnecessary to sew hems in many cases; modern cloth and fibers will generally not permit such liberties in reproduction clothing, so the reader should be prepared to include hems, even though no hems or seam allowances are given in the accompanying illustrations.

It may seem obvious, but it should be said that these patterns were copied from clothes made for specific people, so they are unlikely to fit most modern people without alterations (for example, very few men of George Washington's height today could fit into his clothes; his shoulders, like most shoulders of his day, were narrow). If the reader decides not to seek the services of a competent tailor or seamstress, each item of clothing should be made first out of scrap material, such as old sheets, to make sure of a proper fit. Be prepared to remake some items several times before you achieve success, particularly where the sleeves meet the body of a coat or a gown.

Those who would like to have clothing made for them may search long and hard before finding anyone capable of making accurate period clothing. Therefore, the names of four such people are included here, in alphabetical order, with their addresses correct as of 1990. No warranty as to their work is expressed or implied by their inclusion here, but I have seen some of their work and am impresssed by it.

G. GEDNEY GODWIN, P.O.Box 100, Valley Forge, PA, 19481. He specializes in 18th-century men's military uniforms, but is also able to supply other period clothing.

RICK HAVEN, 319 Oak Tree Road, Williamsburg, VA, 23185. He supplies whatever period clothing required at a reasonable price.

JANICE RYAN, 302 East Main Street, Berryville, VA, 22611. She makes primarily women's clothing of the period 1750–1800.

LYNN SYMBORSKI, 327 Kenmore Road, Havertown, PA, 19083. She makes primarily women's clothing of almost any historical period and can also produce men's clothing of almost any historical period.

If you write to any or all of these people, please enclose a self-addressed, stamped envelope, so that you are more likely to receive a reply. These people are all well-mannered, but they are also extremely busy.

Readers seriously interested in making period clothing are urged to consult more complete and more authoritative books than this one. Here is a list of the best, in alphabetical order.

Janet Arnold, Patterns of Fashion I, c.1660–1860, New York, Drama Books Specialists, 1964.

Doris Edson & Lucy Barton, Period Patterns, Boston, Walter H Baker Co., 1942.

Margot H. Hill & Peter A. Bucknell, The Evolution of Fashion: Pattern & Cut from 1066–1930, New York, Drama Book Publishers, 1967.

Mary M. Johnson et al., Historic Colonial French Dress, West Lafayette, IN, Ouabache Press, 1982.

Robert L. Klinger, Distaff Sketchbook, Union City, TN, Pioneer Press, 1974.

Robert L. Klinger & Richard A. Wilder, Sketchbook 76, Union City, TN, Pioneer Press, 1967.

Carl Kohler, A History of Costume, New York, Dover Publications, 1963/1928.

Norah Waugh, The Cut of Men's Clothes 1600–1900, New York, Theatre Arts Books, 1964.

Norah Waugh, The Cut of Women's Clothes 1600–1930, New York, Theatre Arts Books, 1968.

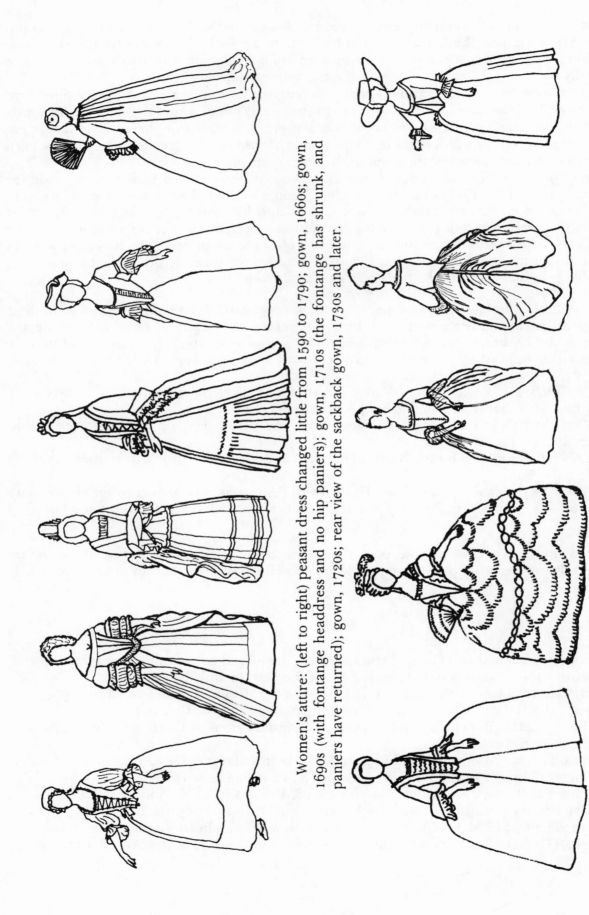

Women's attire: (left to right) peasant dress changed little from 1590 to 1790; gown, 1660s; gown, 1690s (with fontange headdress and no hip paniers); gown, 1710s (the fontange has shrunk, and paniers have returned); gown, 1720s; rear view of the sackback gown, 1730s and later.

Women's attire: (left to right) gown, 1740s (with exaggerated paniers); court ballgown, 1770s; front and rear views of polonaise gown of 1770s; gown, 1780s, showing popular "zone" on bodice.

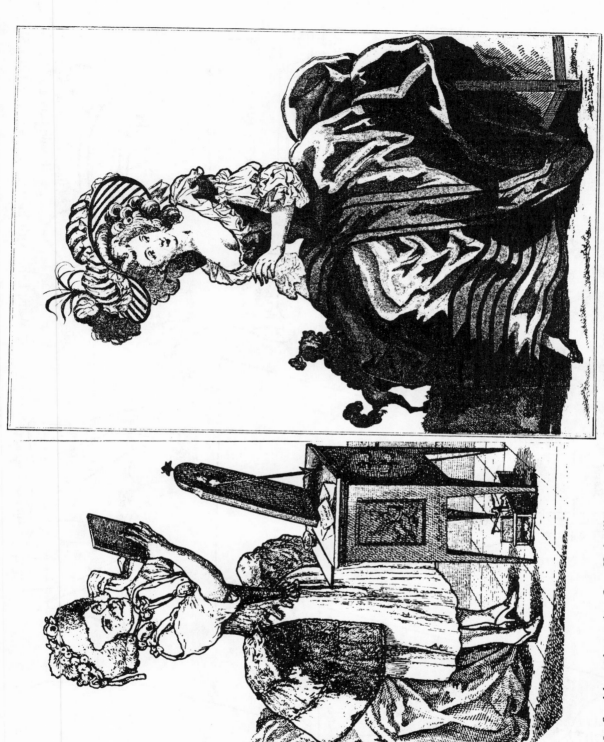

Left: although a pair of stuffed pillowcases hanging on a belt will often suffice for a woman's paniers, the best paniers are light, collapsible steel frames covered with cloth. Right: the 1784 French fashion book, La Galerie des Modes, showed this to be typical of well-dressed women in the United States.

31

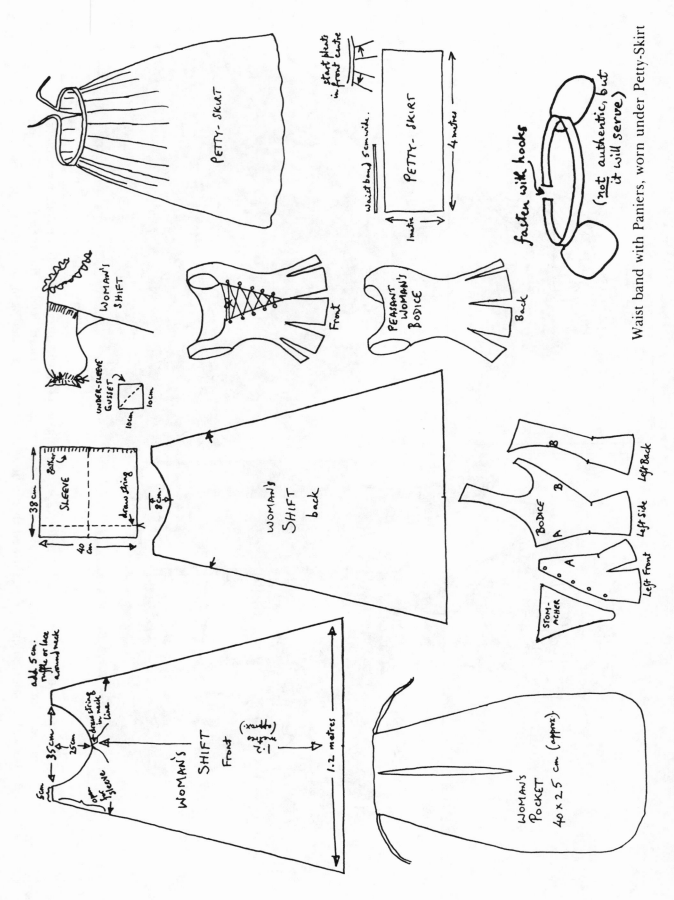

Waist band with Paniers, worn under Petty-Skirt

PETTY-SKIRT

PETTY-SKIRT

4 metres

Waist band 5 cm wide.

1 metre

start pleats in front centre

fasten with hooks

(not authentic, but it will serve)

WOMAN'S SHIFT

Front

PEASANT WOMAN'S BODICE

Back

UNDER-SLEEVE GUSSET

10 cm.

10 cm.

38 cm

40 cm

SLEEVE

Gather

drawing string

8 cm

WOMAN'S SHIFT back

BODICE

A

B

A

Left Front

Left Side

Left Back

STOM-ACHER

add 5 cm. ruffle or lace around neck

35 cm

25 cm

5 cm

drawing string in neck hem

open for sleeve

WOMAN'S SHIFT Front

(xxxtto) as you like it

1.2 metres

WOMAN'S POCKET
40 x 25 cm (approx)

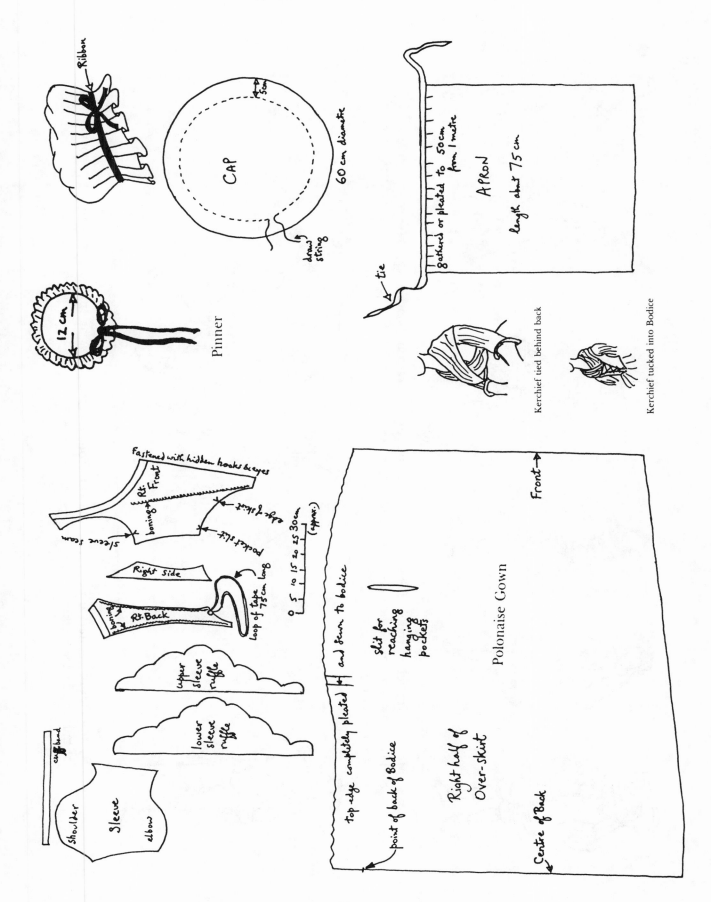

Ribbon

CAP

60 cm diameter

5cm

draw
string

Pinner

12 cm

APRON

length about 75 cm

gathered or pleated to 50cm from 1 metre

tie

Kerchief tied behind back

Kerchief tucked into Bodice

Fastened with hidden hooks & eyes

Rt. Front

boning

sleeve seam

edge of skirt

pocket slit

Right Side

Rt. Back

boning

Loop of tape 75 cm long

0 5 10 15 20 25 30cm (approx.)

upper sleeve ruffle

lower sleeve ruffle

cuff band

Shoulder

Sleeve

elbow

top edge completely pleated and sewn to bodice

point of back of Bodice

slit for reaching hanging pockets

Polonaise Gown

Front →

Right half of Over-skirt

Centre of Back

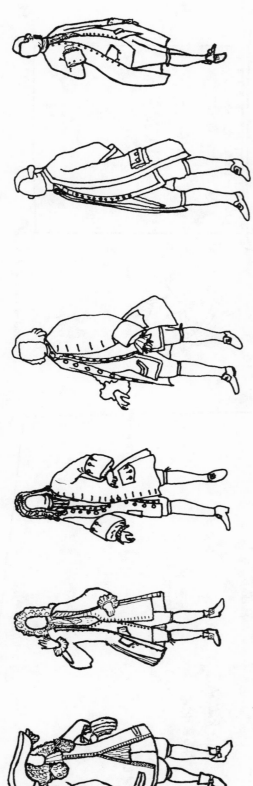

Men's attire: (left to right) 1660s; 1690s; 1720s (buttons are larger and fewer); 1750s (fewer buttons; coat is cut away to reveal the lower waistcoat); 1770s (less cloth in the tail); 1780s (coat more cut away; waistcoat shorter).

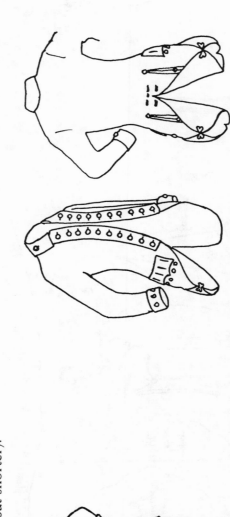

Men's attire: military uniform, 1770s, with front and rear views of uniform coat (note how corners of tails are folded back).

34

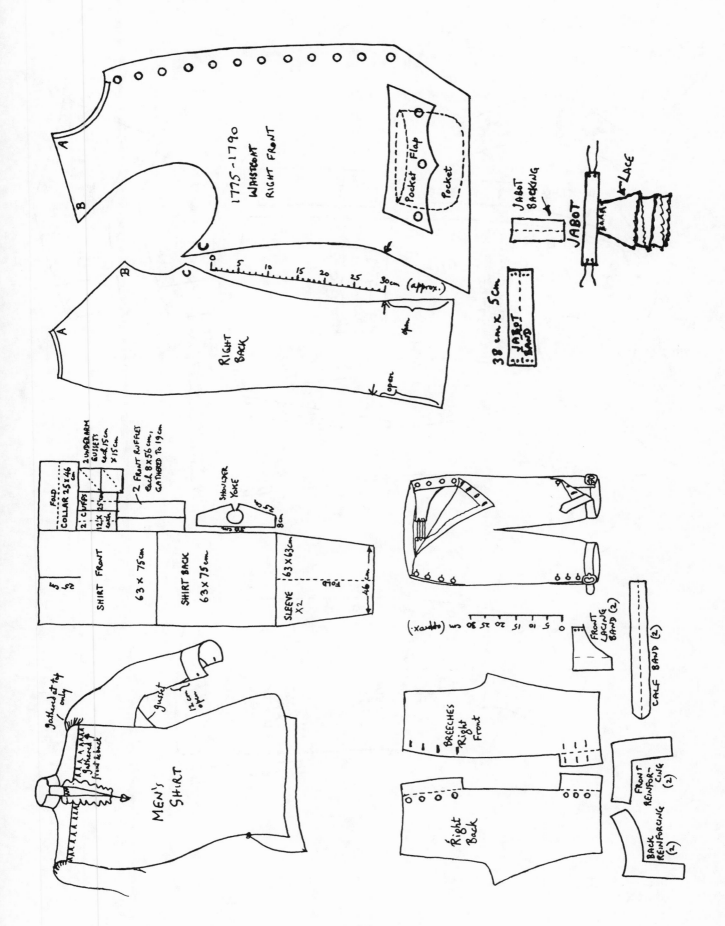

1775-1790
WAISTCOAT
RIGHT FRONT

Pocket Flap
Pocket

RIGHT BACK

0 5 10 15 20 25 30cm (approx.)

open

JABOT BACKING

JABOT

LACE

38 cm x 5 cm
JABOT BAND

FOLD COLLAR 25 x 46 cm

2 UNDERARM GUSSETS each 15cm x 15cm

2 FRONT RUFFLES each 8 x 56 cm, GATHERED TO 19cm

2: CUFFS 17½ x 25cm each

SHOULDER YOKE

SHIRT FRONT 63 x 75cm

SHIRT BACK 63 x 75cm

SLEEVE x 2 63 x 63cm

FOLD

46 cm

Gathered at top only

gusset

12 cm open

Gathered front & back

MEN'S SHIRT

0 5 10 15 20 25 30 cm (approx.)

FRONT LACING BAND (2)

CALF BAND (2)

BREECHES Right Front

Right Back

FRONT REINFORCING (2)

BACK REINFORCING (2)

35

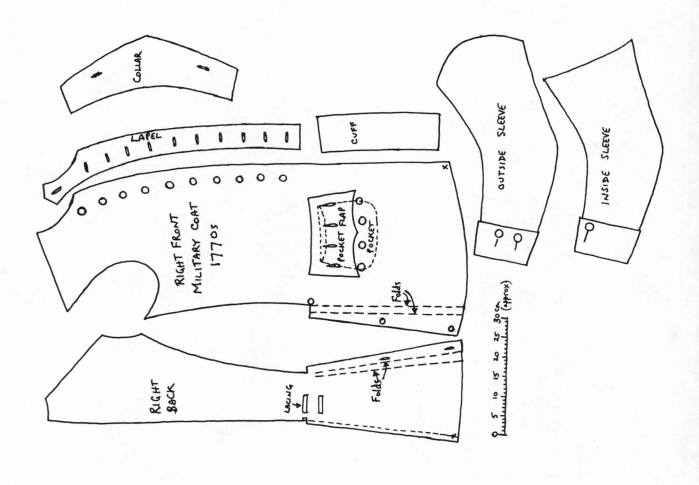

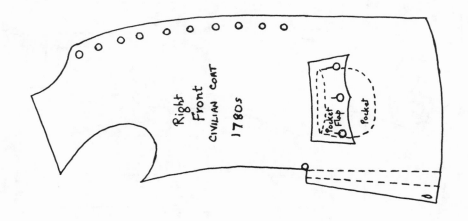

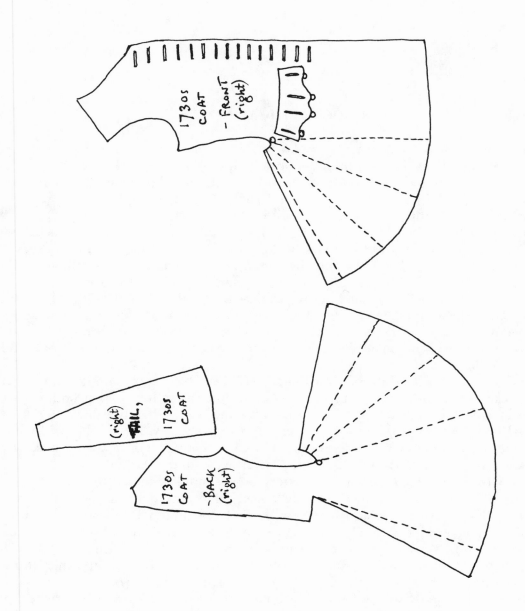

1730s COAT
- FRONT (right)

1730s COAT
- BACK (right)

1730s COAT, TAIL, (right)

BIBLIOGRAPHICAL NOTES

Any study of early American dance and popular music written in the past few decades necessarily owes much to the pioneering—and continuing—work of Kate Van Winkle Keller. A few of her most important works are mentioned here: (with Carolyn Rabson), The National Tune Index (in microfiche), New York, University Music Editions, 1980; "A Bibliography of Eighteenth-century American Social Dance," Country Dance & Song, vol.18, Spring, 1988; (with Joy Van Cleef), "Selected American Country Dances and Their English Sources," Music in Colonial Massachusetts, vol.1, Boston, The Colonial Society of Massachusetts, 1980; "John Griffiths, Eighteenth-Century Itinerant Dancing Master," Itinerancy in New England, Boston, Boston University, 1986 (the article has since been republished as a separate pamphlet by the Henderson Group, Sandy Hook, CT); (with Ralph Sweet), A Choice Selection of American Country Dances of the Revolutionary Era 1775-1795, New York, Country Dance & Song Society, 1976; Kate Keller's essay on and edition of the 1730 James Alexander dance manuscript in the New-York Historical Society is soon to be published in Israel J. Katz, ed., Libraries, History, Diplomacy & the Performing Arts: Essays in Honor of Carleton Sprague Smith, New York Public Library.

Somehow Kate Keller's husband, Robert M. Keller, has been able to take enough time out from his busy schedule as an important regulatory official of the nuclear industry to produce a work only slightly less important than the National Tune Index for the study of early American dance. This is Dance Figures Index: American Country Dances 1730-1810, Sandy Hook, CT, the Hendrickson Group, 1989. The Hendrickson Group was founded by Cyril "Chip" Hendrickson, whose book, Early American Dance & Music: John Griffiths, Dancing Master, 29 Country Dances, 1788, was published by the Hendrickson Group in 1989. One further modern book should be mentioned: James E. Morrison (former Director of the Country Dance & Song Society), Twenty-Four Early American Country Dances, Cotillions & Reels for the Year 1976, New York, The Country Dance & Song Society, 1976.

The rest of these notes will be divided into five categories. First, British and other European dance books published 1651-1800; second, North American dance books published 1788-1810; third, manuscript dance books, mostly North American, from 1730-1810; fourth, published music books; and fifth, manuscript tune books, mostly North American, from 1720-1810.

European dance published books (all published in London, except where otherwise indicated): Bride, ca.1782; Budd, ca.1800; Cahusac, ca.1800; Caledonian Country Dances, 1754; Cantelo, 1785 (a book of 24 country dances as danced by British troops in New York, Philadelphia, Newport, Charleston and Savannah during the War of Independence); Johnson/Wright I, 1740; Johnson/Wright II, 1742; Johnson III, 1744; Johnson IV, 1748; Johnson V, 1750; Johnson VI, 1751; Longman, 1781; Markordt (12 Contredansen voor de Viool en Dwars Fluyt . . ., Amsterdam), 1771; Neal (Dublin), 1726; Playford and Playford/Young, about 27 editions from 1651 to about 1727; Rutherford I, 1750; Rutherford II/1, 1756; Rutherford II/2, 1760; Skillern, 1780; Thompson, 16 editions from 1757 to 1800; Walsh, 6 editions from 1718 to 1747; Wilson, various editions in the first three decades of the 19th century.

American published dance books (in chronological order): John Griffiths, A Collection of the newest & most fashionable   Country Dances & Cotillions, Providence, 1788; Philo-Musico (pseud.), "Columbia, A New Country Dance," The Massachusetts Magazine, Feb., 1790, Boston; Young's Vocal & Instrumental Musical Miscellany, Philadelphia, 1793; Griffiths II, Northampton, MA, 1794; A New Academy of Complements . . . , Worcester, 1795; Fraisier, The Scholars Companion, Boston, 1796; American Ladies Pocket Book, Philadelphia, 1796; W— D—, An Elegant Collection . . . , Amherst, MA, 1798; A New Collection of Country Dances, Leominster, MA, 1799; Fisin, Ode to May, New York, 1799; American Ladies Pocket Book, Philadelphia, 1799; Saltator (pseud.), A treatise on Dancing . . . I, Boston, 1802; Saltator II, Boston, 1807; Blanchard, A Collection of the Most Celebrated . . . , Windsor, VT, 1809. Several further books on dance were published in America in this period, but most of them are derivative from the others or from various British books.

Manuscript dance books: other than the Alexander manuscript mentioned above, the earliest survivor is a book primarily of cotillions and tune incipits from Trois Rivieres, Quebec, ca.1765; after that, the earliest is now lost: a 1781 book by Miss Champlin of Newport, RI, quoted in George Champlin Mason, Reminiscences of Newport, 1884; the Weeks MS (Greenland, NH, 1783); The First Assembly (Philadelphia, 1783); the Frobischer MS (Montreal, 1793); the Muzzey MS (Plainfield, VT, 1795); the Shepley MS (Pepperrell, MA, 1794); the Arnold MS (Providence, 1790s); the Willcox MS (Hartford, 1793); the Moore-Ridgely MS (Dover, DE, 1790s); the Roth MS (Philadelphia, 1790). In addition, the Turner tune book contains one set of dance directions.

Published tune books: one dance each was taken from the Hurlbert Fife Book, Moller & Capron's Monthly Numbers no.3 (Philadelphia, 1793), and Ralph's operetta, The Fashionable Lady.

Manuscript tune books: among the most important are the Parkman MS (Boston, 1721), the earliest references to specific dances in America; the Turner MS (Norwich, CT, 1788), which is closely related to the Griffiths I dance book, 1788 (see above) and to Griffiths' lost dance book published at New Haven in 1786; the Murphey MS (Newport, 1790); and the Carroll MS, (ca.1800, original place unknown, now at the Newberry Library in Chicago); other manuscripts consulted are (in alphabetical order): Aborn; Adams; W.Allen; Beck; Cary; Cunningham; Eels; Gaylord; Greenwood; Hawkins; Nivison; Peirce; Perkins; Shattuck; Skipwith and others that are anonymous. All these are fully described in the National Tune Index (mentioned above), except for the Skipwith MS (Virginia, 1790s), a copy of which is at the University of Virginia Library.

Top: The Dancing Schoole; when Henry Playford took over from his late father in 1686 he had this frontispiece engraved for subsequent editions of The Dancing Master. Middle: When John Young took over from Henry Playford in 1728 he had this frontispiece engraved for a one-time use, showing a dance assembly. Bottom: this is believed to have been engraved about 1710 as the frontispiece for a now-lost book of dances by Wright published by Johnson; note the refreshments waiting in the hatch to the left.

COURT and COUNTRY DANCES

Top: Court and Country Dances, frontispiece engraved for Walsh's books of dances about 1710; the dancing couples are leading onto the floor; note the fontanges or high headdresses worn by the women. Bottom: The Village Assembly, a longways dance, by Matthew Darly, 1776.

Frontispieces from various editions of the Thompson dance books.
Top: published about 1760.   Bottom: this is essentially the same
picture in mirror image, but with the clothing updated to the 1780s.

Top: A longways dance at Wanstead House, Essex in the mid-1750s, by Hogarth; the man on the far left is the future George III as a teenager; Wanstead house, one of the great houses of England, was designed by Colen Campbell in 1714 and demolished 1824. Bottom: a triple-minor longways dance by moonlight drawn by Thomas Rowlandson in the 1790s to represent a scene from Goldsmith's 1766 novel, The Vicar of Wakefield; the Paul Mellon Collection, the Yale Center for British Art.

Two sketches by Thomas Rowlandson of longways dances, both about 1790. Bottom: a ball in the great Assembly Room at Bath; Yale Center for British Art, the Paul Mellon Collection.

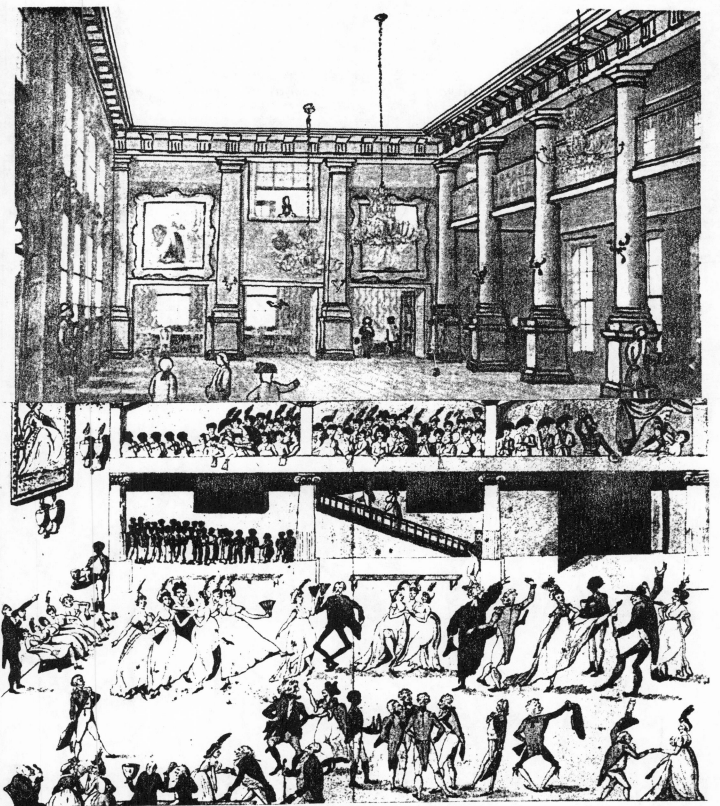

Two views of the large ballroom at the King's House (Governor's Mansion) at Spanish Town, Jamaica. The house was built in 1762, probably to designs by Peter Harrison, and the front wall still stands after the rest of the house was destroyed by fire. Top: from an oil painting by Philip Wickstead, about 1780; the Institute of Jamaica. Bottom: "A Grand Jamaica Ball," engraved by William Holland after a drawing by A. James about 1802; the artist endowed the dancers with abundant character at the expense of an accurate portrayal of the actual dance, and he treated the architecture with no greater accuracy.

Top: a Scots reel, by Matthew Darly, 1776 (one of five known early pictures of the Scots Reel), related to the dance "The Gordian Knot." Bottom: Virginia slaves doing a longways country dance to the music of what is probably a cittern (English guitar), fiddle and bones; watercolor by Lewis Miller, 1853, Abby Aldrich Folk Art Center, Williamsburg; With minor changes of clothing, this scene would have been entirely appropriate 75 years earlier.

Top: a circular dance for as many as will (like Sellenger's Round) but with a couple embracing in the middle. Because such dances do not appear in dance books after about 1700 it is widely assumed that they were no longer danced by then, but this detail from an anonymous engraving of revels on Greenwich Hill outside London ca.1755 shows otherwise. Bottom: "The Cotillion Dance," engraved after John Collet about 1770, Colonial Williamsburg Foundation.

Two cotillions. Top: the Duchess of Devonshire at a ball at Windsor about 1778. Bottom: a Paris ball given by Monsieur de Villemorien Tila, by A. de Saint-Aubin ca.1770.

Top: A cotillion, detail from an engraving of a fancy-dress ball at the French court, ca.1783; one bystander is dressed as a Turk and another is wearing 16th-century attire. Bottom: A maypole dance, detail from a 1751 engraving after a now-lost oil painting by Canaletto of a fancy-dress party at Ranelagh Gardens, London; among the dancers are people dressed as a dance master, a hunchback, a harlequin (clown) and a Chinaman, and among the spectators are people dressed as a nun playing a tabor, the Pope, a kilted Scotsman (kilts were outlawed at that time, following Bonnie Prince Charlie's Rebellion in 1745), a Jacobean man, Punch, a sailor, an Elizabethan man, a bishop and several clergy (many not shown in this detail).

49

Sir Foplings Airs.

Joseph Downs Collection of Ephemera

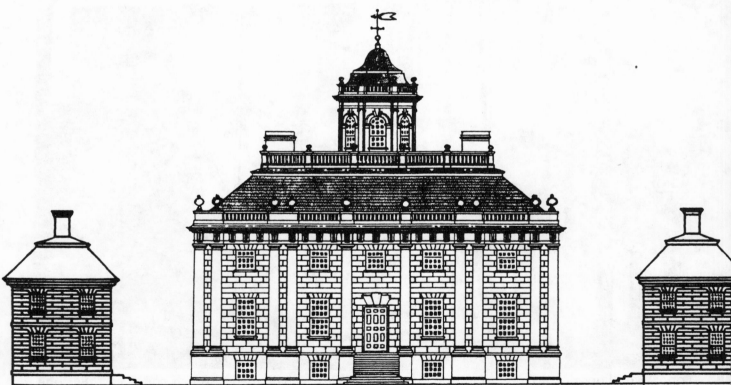

   Top: anonymous caricature of an English longways dance ca.1700 (several decades before the work of the "father of caricature," William Hogarth). The people sitting at the head of the set are probably serving as "the presence." Henry Francis duPont Winterthur Museum. Bottom: the author's elevation drawing of the probable appearance of the entrance front of Shirley Place, Roxbury, MA, designed by Peter Harrison in 1746 with a magnificent 2-storey ballroom. The house still stands, but in unrecognizable form.

Top: the grand ballroom at the Jeremiah Lee Mansion, Marblehead, MA, designed by Peter Harrison in the 1750s and open to the public; copyright 1982, Steve Rosenthal. Bottom: the ballroom built by French officers stationed at Newport, RI 1780–1 next door to Rochambeau's headquarters on Clarke Street. The building still stands in greatly altered form as a house; old photo, Newport Historical Society.

Top: the Long Gallery at the Statehouse, Philadelphia, scene of many balls; Independence National Historical Park Collection. Bottom: the larger of the two ballrooms at Gadsby's Tavern, Alexandria, VA, where George Washington is known to have danced; note the musicians' gallery on the left.

Top: the Great Hall or ballroom, Stratford Hall, Virginia, possibly one of Peter Harrison's earliest designs, ca. 1739, and open to the public; photograph by Richard Cheek, courtesy of the Robert E. Lee Memorial Association, Stratford Hall Plantation. Bottom: the Great Hall or ballroom, Drayton Hall Plantation, near Charleston, SC, built ca. 1738 probably to designs by Peter Harrison, and open to the public; its owners, the National Trust, call it "the most beautiful house in America."

To be sold at this Office,
An elegant Sett of

Watson's Horace.

ALSO may be had at said Office,
A Collection of FIGURES of the
Newest and most Fashoinable

Country Dances.

Newport, June 27, 1788.

A grand BALL.

MR. GRIFFITHS begs Leave to present his most respectful Compliments to the LADIES and GENTLEMEN of Providence, and its Vicinity, and sollicits the Honour of their Company at a GRAND BALL, at Hacker's Hall, on the Evening of the Fourth Day of July, Seven o'Clock, to celebrate the ANNIVERSARY of the INDEPENDENCE OF AMERICA, and the ADOPTION OF THE FEDERAL CONSTITUTION BY NINE STATES. He flatters himself that their Attendance will be general, to testify their Joy on so auspicious an Event. Good Music will be provided, and the Hall well illuminated.

Providence, June 27, 1788.

Top: the advertisement in the New Haven Chronicle for John Griffiths' (now lost) first dance book, published in 1786. Bottom: Griffiths' advertisement in the Providence Gazette for a ball to celebrate the ratification of the United States Constitution, even though Rhode Island was not to ratify for nearly another two years.

A

COLLECTION

OF

The newest and most fashionable

COUNTRY DANCES

AND

COTILLIONS.

The greater Part by

Mr. *JOHN GRIFFITH*, DANCING-MASTER, in *Providence*

COUNTRY DANCES.

No. 1. *The Pleasure of Love.*

HANDS across—back again—cast off two Co.—up again at Top—lead down the Middle—up again, and cast off one Co.—six Hands round—back again.

No. 2. *The Pleasure of Providence.*

Cast off two Co.—come at Top through the Middle, and set—second and third Co.—Hands across—back again—first Co. lead down the Middle—up again—cast off one Co.—right and left at Top.

No. 3. *The Fantocini.*

First and second Co. change Sides—back again—lead down the Middle—up again—cast off one Co.—Hands cross with the third Co.—back again—allemand with your Partner—so back again.

No. 4. *The new Russia Dance.*

First Lady sets to the second Gentleman—go back and turn both single—the Gentleman does the same—then the two Ladies balance to each other—at the same Time the two Gentlemen do the same—the first and second Co. balance to each other—Hands four round—lead down the Middle—up again—cross over—right and left at Top.

No. 5. *The Morning Gazette.*

The first Co. set to the second Lady, then to the second Gentleman lead down the Middle—up again, and cast off.

No. 6.

No. 12. Morris's Dance.

The first Lady turns the second Gent. quite round—first Gent. does the same with the second Lady—lead down the Middle—up again, and cast off one Co.—turn your Partner with your right Hand, Halfway—back again, with the left Hand—six Hands round—Halfway—back again.

No. 13. First of May.

First and second Co. chassee out—two Ladies together, and two Gent. the same—back again—lead down the Middle—up again, and cast off one Co.—the Gent. chassee to his Partner's Side—his Partner does the same to his Side—back again.

No. 14. Maid of the Oaks.

First Lady sets to the second Gent.—turns the third, and goes to her former Place—the first Gent. sets to the second Lady, turns the third, and remains between the third Co. and his Partner between the second Co.—balance all six—set—turn your Partner with your right Hand, and turn until you are between the second and third Ladies—balance again—set, and return to your Places.

No. 15. Poor Soldier.

The first Lady balances to the second Gentleman—sets and turns him quite round—goes to her former Place—the first Gent. does the same with the second Lady—lead down the Middle—up again, and cast off one Co.—the first Gent. takes both Hands to the third Gent.—chassee out—back again—the first Lady does the same with the third Lady.

No. 16. Quesnay.

The first Co. lead down the Middle—up again, set and cast off back, and go at Top—the third Co. lead up, set at Top, and cast off—go to their former Places—first Co. cross over the second and third Co.—the first Lady crosses between the first and second Gent.—the Gent. does the

No. 6. Trio.

First and second Set balance opposite to each other Set—then four Hands round—so back again—lead down the Middle—up again, cast off one Co.—chassee to your Partners Places—and back again.

No. 7. Miss Arnold's Delight.

Cast off two Co.—up again—second and third Co.—four Hands round—back again—first Co. lead down the Middle—up again—and cast off one Co.—turn your Partner with your right Hand—so back again with the left.

No. 8. La Bagatelle.

First Co. set to the second Lady, and turn all three quite round—do the same with the second Gentleman—lead down the Middle—up again—and cast off one Co.—turn your Partner with one Hand—back again.

No. 9. The Groves.

Cross Hands—back again—lead down the Middle—up again, and cast off one Co.—four Hands round—back again—right and left at Top.

No. 10. Nosegay.

First and second Ladies give Hands—change to the Gentlemens Side—the Gent. do the same to the Ladies Side—back again—lead down the Middle—up again, and cast off one Co.—cross Hands with the third Co. Halfway—back again—right and left at Top.

No. 11. Constancy.

Cross Hands—back again—lead down the Middle—up again, and cast off one Co.—balance all six—turn your Partner quite round, and right and left at Top.

No. 12.

the fame between the firft and fecond Ladies)—then turn your Partner with your right Hand, between the firft and fecond Co.—right and left at Top.

No. 17. Griffith's *Whim.*

Turn your Partner with the right Hand Halfway, and fet—lead down until you are between the firft and fecond Co.—then caft off back—go at Top—the fecond Co. do the fame, and caft off the third Co.—then balance all four—fet—Hands crofs at Top—Halfway fet—then Half right and left at Top.

No. 18. M. La Fayette.

Firft Lady paffes between the fecond and third Co.—fets between third and fourth Co.—the Gent. does the fame between the fecond and third Ladies, and fets between the third and fourth Co.—come at Top—the Lady croffes between the fecond and third Ladies, and her Partner does the fame by croffing between the fecond and third Gent.—four Hands round at Top—Halfway—back again—lead down the Middle—up again, and caft off one Co.—fet—fix Hands round—back again.

No. 19. *Lady Buckley's Whim.*

Caft off two Co.—up again—lead down the Middle, and up again—then caft off one Co.—the Lady ftands between the fecond Co.—and the Gent. between the third Co.—balance in the Middle all fix—turn your Partner with the right Hand, Halfway—fet—fix Hands round—back again—right and left at Top.

No. 20. Fifher's *Hornpipe.*

Caft off back—up again—lead down the Middle—up again, and caft off one Co.—Hands crofs at Bottom—Halfway—back again—right and left at Top.

No. 21.

57

No. 21. *New Star.*

Turn your Partner with your right Hand quite round—then caft off two Co.—fet—come at Top through the Middle, and fet at Top—then caft off one Co.—fix Hands round—Halfway, and back again.

No. 22. *The Ifle of Sky.*

-- Caft off two Co.—back again—lead down the Middle—up again, and caft off one Co.—chaffee to the Ladies Side, and the Ladies to the Gent. Side.

No. 23. Nightingale's *Fancy.*

Caft off two Co.—up again—lead down the Middle—up again, and caft off one Co.—firft and fecond chaffee out—fet—back again—then four Hands round at Top—Halfway, and back again.

No. 24. Griffith's *Fancy.*

Crofs Hands—back again—the Lady paffes behind the fecond Gent.—and the Gent. does the fame behind the fecond Lady—fet, and turn your Partner Halfway between the fecond and third Co.—four Hands round—back again—right and left at Top.

No. 25. Cameron's *Rant.*

Caft off two Co.—up again—lead down the Middle—up again, and caft off one Co.—turn Corners, and take your Partner—draw her to her Side—fet, and to your Side.

No. 26. *The young Widow.*

Crofs Hands—back again—lead down the Middle, then turn your Partner up again, and caft off the Gent. cafts off one Co. to the Ladies Side, and the Lady to the Gent. Side—balance all fix—fet, and go all round—fecond and third Co. balance in the Middle, oppofite to each other—then Half right and left in the Middle.

No. 27.

No. 27. The Whimfical Lady.

Turn your Partner with one Hand--fo back again--lead down the Middle--up again, and caft of one Co.--turn Corners--back again--take your Partner with both Hands--draw her to you Side--fo back again.

No. 28. Washington's Refignation.

Turn your Partner Halfway--back again--lead down the Middle--up again--caft of one Co.--fix Hands round--back again--lead out fide--back again.

No. 29. The Lover in Diftrefs.

Firft Gent. croffes between the fecond and third Ladies--the Lady does the fame--and the Gent. croffes between the fecond and third Gent.--come at Top--lead down the Middle--balance all fix--then turn your Partner quite round--chaffee to the Gent. Side--back again.

COTILLIONS.

No. 1. The Forty-fecond.

All round, Halfway--back again--the firft and fecond Co. meet together--fet and chaffee Halfway--then ftand ftill--the third and fourth Co. do the fame--firft and fecond Co. chaffee back--fet. and turn their Partners quite round with one Hand--fet--third and fourth Co. do the fame.

No. 2. The Happy Meeting.

All round, Halfway--back again--two oppofite Co. balance--fet--take contrary Partners--crofs between the third and fourth Co. and come to their Places--third and fourth Co. do the fame--all eight chaffee--fet and turn contrary Partners--chaffee back and turn contrary Co. do the fame.

No. 3.

No. 3. The Academy Cotillion.

All round Halfway--back again--then form two Lines--balance all eight opposite to each other--fet--then clap Hands--take opposite Partners--draw quite round--chaffee back again--turn quite round--oppofite Partners--four Ladies balance in the Middle--fet--right and left--back again.

No. 4. La Tracie.

All round, and back again--the firft Gent. and the oppofite Lady change Places--then chaffee, and back again--then lead up--balance Rigadoon, and turn with both Hands into their Places--the other three Co. do the fame.

No. 5. La Petite Province.

All round--back again--the firft and oppofite Co. lead up--balance Rigadoon--Hands acrofs, Half round, and turn your Partners in contrary Places--the other two Co. do the fame--promenade in their own Places--chaffee all eight.

No. 6. La Fayette.

All round--back again--crofs Hands four each Corner--back again--firft and oppofite Co. face to the third and fourth Co. and change Places with the oppofite Co.--fet--the third and fourth Co. do the fame--fet--then right and left all round unto your former Places,

No. 7. La Beauté.

All round, and back again--all four Co. chaffee--... promenade round in the ...--the fourth Gent. ... the firft and third Co. balance and rigadoon--take their ... Partners with both Hands and turn them, but not in their own Places--the other two Co. do the fame--then grand Moline into their own Places.

No. 8.

No. 8. La Jeuneffe.

All round--back again--the first and opposite Co. balance Rigadoon, and turn each other's Partners quite round--go back again into their own Places--the other two Co. do the same--chaffee all eight, and turn contrary Partners--chaffee back again, and turn contrary Partners--then the fourth Co. form two Lines--balance Rigadoon--Hands across, both Sides--Half round in the contrary Places--then balance again by two Lines--Hands across--back again--and go to their Places.

No. 9. Les Folies Dames.

All round--back again--first and opposite Co. lead up to the right Hand Side Co.--balance Rigadoon, and change Places with their Partners in their Hands--the other two Co. do the same--promenade in their own Places--chaffee all eight--back again.

No. 10. Les Paniers.

All round, and back again--the first and opposite Co. turn single. Half round, and back again--then balance--turn each other's Partners into contrary Places--then turn as before--balance and turn each other's Partners with both Hands into their own Places--the second Co. do the same.

No. 11. La Delice.

All round, and back again--the first and opposite Co. lead up, then lead up with contrary Partners to the Side Co.--turn with your right Hand the opposite Lady, and back again with the left--and go back to your former Places--the other two Co. do the same--the first and opposite Co. change Places, and turn their Partners with both Hands--the other two Co. do the same--promenade into your own Places--all eight--back again.

No. 12. La Charlotte.

All round, and back again--the Ladies promenade round to the Left, and the Gentlemen to the Right--balance Rigadoon to contrary Partners.

Partners, and turn with both Hands--chaffee all eight--back again--then the four Ladies and four Gentlemen go on as before, till they come into contrary Places--then balance Rigadoon to their own Partners, and turn with both Hands--chaffee all eight--the four Ladies lead up in the Center--balance Rigadoon--Hands across Half round--at the same Time the Gent. promenade round single, and meet their Partners--then the four Gent. lead up in the Center, Hands across Halfway--at the same Time the four Ladies promenade round, and meet their Partners, fo that they come into contrary Places as before--then promenade into their own Places.

No. 13. Morris's Cotillion.

First and opposite Co. turn contrary Partners with their right Hands--stand still--the third and fourth Co. do the same--chaffee all eight back again--right and left, until you get to your former Places.

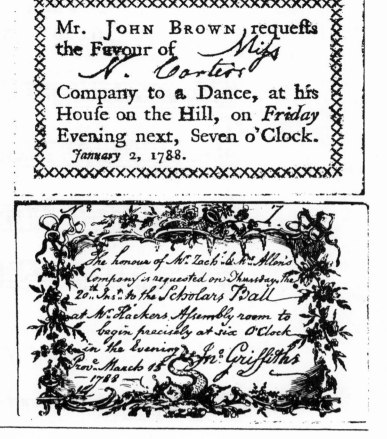

Mr. JOHN BROWN, requests the Favour of *Miss N. Carter's* Company to a Dance, at his House on the Hill, on *Friday* Evening next, Seven o'Clock.
January 2, 1788.

The honour of Mr. Zach: & Mrs. Allen's Company is requested on Thursday, the 20th Inst. to the Scholars Ball at Mr. Hackers Affembly room to begin precisely at six O'Clock in the evening. Jno Griffiths
Provce March 15 1788

Fisher's *Hornpipe.*
(LORD HOWE'S HORNPIPE)

Maid of the Oaks.

The young Widow.

THE DANCES: LONGWAYS
(in alphabetical order)

A number of dances, that might otherwise have been included, do not appear in this book, because they have already been published, or are about to be published in other popular works. These dances are listed here, and their respective books may be purchased (when available) from the Country Dance & Song Society in Northampton, Massachusetts.

James E. Morrison, Twenty Four Early American Country Dances, Cotillions & Reels for the Year 1976, The Country Dance & Song Society, 1976. Contents: Bonny Lass of Aberdeen, The Convention Cotillion, The Doubtful Shepherd, Elegance & Simplicity, Four Hand Reel, The Innocent Maid, Jockey to the Fair, Maid of the Oaks, Marlbrouk Cotillion, Mr. Turner's Academy Cotillion, Money in Both Pockets, Pea Straw, Revenge, The Rose Tree, Six Hand Reel, Stony Point, Stony Point, Three Hand Reel, The Virginia Reel of 1801, Yankee Doodle; The Young Widow.

Kate VanWinkle Keller and Ralph Sweet: A Choice Selection of American Country Dances of the Revolutionary Era, 1775–1795, The Country Dance & Song Society, 1976. Contents: Allemande Swiss, Ashley's Ride, Barrel of Sugar, La Belle Catherine, The Black Joke, College Hornpipe, The Dusty Miller, The Duchess of Brunswick, Fisher's Hornpipe (Lord Howe's Hornpipe), Flowers of Edinburgh, German Spa, Greensleeves, Hunt the Squirrel, Hessian Dance, The Irish Wash Woman, Lady's Breast Knot, The Lily, Love Forever, Love in a Village, Maid of the Mill, Miss Moore's Rant, Nancy Dawson, Over the Hills & Far Away, Rural Felicity, Saint Patrick's Day in the Morning, Soldier's Joy, A Successful Campaign, Sukey Bids Me, Sweet Richard.

Kate VanWinkle Keller, (title uncertain) The Alexander Manuscript, 1730, due to be published ca.1991. Contents: Wooden Shoe, Bartholomew's Fair, Lane's Minuet, The Knot, Richmond Ball, Moth Q Loge, Prince Eugene's March, Virgin 15 Years, Jig, Colliers Daughter, Valentine's Day, Jenny Come t'Ye, Grounds Greensleeves, Christ's Church Bells, Some Say the Devil's Dead, Betty Fair, Spanheim, Young Roger, The Recruiting Officer, Shawberry Park, Marlborough's Victory, The Dusty Miller, The Gunfleet, Devil Take Wars, Durn You, Happy.

ADMIRAL RODNEY'S DELIGHT
24-bar duple-minor longways; moderate.
dance & tune: Thompson; Rodney defeated De Grasse in 1782, so that Britain could claim she had defeated France while losing America.

1-8	1s cast off in 8 counts (2s move up on counts 5–8); partners turn once around with 2 hands.
9-16	1s and 2s dance a right-hand star and a left-hand star back.
17-24	1s and 2s dance rights & lefts, four changes, starting with partners facing.

ADMIRAL RODNEY'S TRIUMPH
32-bar duple-minor longways; moderate.
dance & tune: Bride, ca.1782.

1-8	Partners set and change sides, set and change back again.
9-16	1s go down the middle, come back and cast off (2s moving up).
17-24	Partners allemande right and then allemande left.
25-32	1s and 2s dance rights & lefts, four changes, starting with partners facing.

AMERICA

24-bar duple-minor longways; moderate-easy.

dance & tune: Playford 11th edition, 1701; this dance, which also sometimes had a minuet section inthe middle, was so popular that it continued to be published well after mid-century by Thompson.

1s set and cast down below 2s; set and cast back up.

1s cross & cast (2s move up) and dance half a figure-8 up through the 2s.

1s and 2s circle to the left and circle back to the right.

THE ANSPACHER

24-bar duple-minor longways; moderate.

dance & tune: Cantelo, 1785. Cantelo (no first name yet known) was a dance master with the British troops in America during the War of Independence, and he published in London a book of dances danced by the British officers in New York, Philadelphia and Charleston, and presumably in such other bases as Newport and Savannah. An Anspacher was a member of one of the German mercenary troops fighting for the British in America.

1-8	1s and 2s dance a right-hand star and a left-hand star back.
9-16	1s cross & cast (2s move up) and turn one and a half times around with 2 hands to proper sides.
17-24	1s and 2s dance rights & lefts, four changes, starting with partners facing.

ARCADIAN NUPTIALS

24-bar (a slipjig, triple-time) triple-minor longways; moderate.
dance & tune: Thompson; this is one of the three dances described as having been danced at the Turtle Frolic, Newport, 1752, many years before it was actually published.

1-8	1s turn by the right and cast off into 2nd place (2s move up). 1s turn by the left once around and cast oppositely, the man down around the 3 man to stand between the 3s facing up, and the woman up around the 2 woman to stand between the 2s facing down.
9-16	Taking hands in lines of 3 across the set, all set twice; during the second setting, the 1s turn single as they move over to stand between the 2s and 3s on the improper sides; taking hands on the sides, all set twice.
17-24	All 3 couples circle once around to the left, and then partners turn with 2 hands (the 1s turn once and a half around to return to proper sides; others turn once around).

LA BAGATELLE (The Flirtation)

32-bar duple-minor longways; moderate.
dance: Griffiths I, 1788; tune: Gallini.

1-8	1s set twice to the 2 woman, then all 3 circle once around to the left.
9-16	1s repeat with the 2 man.
17-24	1s go down the middle, come back and cast off (2s moving up).
25-32	Partners turn by the right, then turn by the left.

BALTIMORE
24-bar duple-minor longways; moderate
dance: Moore/Ridgely, 1790s; tune: Carroll MS.

 X1

 X2

1-8	Men face down and women face up; all chasser 4 steps across the set (partners passing face to face); rigadoon, chasser back and rigadoon.
9-16	1s go down the middle, come back and cast off (2s moving up).
17-24	1s and 2s dance rights & lefts, four changes, starting with partners facing.

BARBADOS
32-bar duple-minor longways; moderate.
dance & tune: Johnson III.

1-8	1s cast down the outside for 6 counts and come back up for 2 counts into 2nd place (the 2s having moved up immediately); partners turn once around with 2 hands.
9-16	1s dance a full figure-8 up through the 2s.
17-24	First corners set; second corners set; take hands on the sides and all set twice.
25-32	1s and 2s dance rights & lefts, four changes, starting with partners facing.

BARON STEUBEN
36-bar triple or duple-minor longways; moderate-difficult.
dance: Willcox MS, 1793; tune: Carroll MS; Friedrich Wilhelm Augustus Baron von Steuben volunteered for the American cause in the War of Independence and he was made the general in charge of training/drilling the troops, a great help in winning the war.

1-8	1s lead down through the 2s (who move or cast up immediately); 1s face up and 2s face down; partners take hands and set twice; partners face and set once.
9-16	1s and 2s circle to the left and circle back to the right.
17-20	All set twice.
21-28	2 man, followed by 1 man (and 3 man if a triple) cast off and continue in a small circle or "run-around" back to places. Then the 2 woman leads the women in a similar figure.
29-36	Men face down and women face up; all chasser 4 steps across the set (partners passing face to face); balancer; chasser back; balancer.

THE BEAUX' DELIGHT
32-bar duple-minor longways; moderate.
dance & tune: Playford 11th edition, 1701; tune in Parkman MS, 1721, the earliest American document containing dance tunes. Ebenezer Parkman was a Congregationalist minister in the Boston area.

1-8	1s dance half a figure-8 down through the 2s; all turn single (cloverleaf); 1s (in 4 counts) cast, cross back to proper sides (2s move up immediately).
9-16	2s do what the 1s did.
17-24	1s pattacake and cast off (2s move up); 2s pattacake and cast off (1s move up).
25-32	Three changes of a circular hey; 1s lead up and cast off.

66

LA BELLE ANNETTE
32-bar triple or duple-minor longways; moderate.
dance & tune: Cantelo, 1785.

1-8	1s and 2s dance a right-hand star and a left-hand star back.
9-16	1s cross over 2 couples (cross by the right, cast, cross over again by the right and cast again to below the 2nd standing couple).
17-24	1s lead up to the top (it is permissible to turn with 2 hands on the way up to fill the music, or perhaps use the bourree step) and cast off (2s move up).
25-32	Partners balancer and allemande right half way around; then balancer and allemande left back.

THE BELLES ABOUT THE FLAT BUSH (a Village on Long Island so called)
32-bar duple-minor longways; moderate.
dance & tune: Cantelo, 1785.

1-8	1s and 2s dance a right-hand star and a left-hand star back.
9-16	1s go down the outside for 8 counts, turn and come back.
17-24	1s turn with 2 hands half way around and back, then lead down the middle for 8 counts.
25-32	1s turn with 2 hands once around, lead quickly up to the top and cast off (2s move up).

THE BELLS OF NEWPORT/THE BELLES OF NEW-YORK

32-bar triple or duple-minor longways; moderate.
dance: [New York] The Gentleman & Lady's Companion, 1798–9; tune: [Newport] Murphey MS, 1790.

1-8	1s and 2s dance a right-hand star and a left-hand star back.
9-16	1s go down the middle, come back and cast off (2s moving up).
17-24	1s and the couple below circle to the left and circle back to the right.
25-32	1s and 2s dance rights & lefts, four changes, starting with partners facing.

BILL OF RIGHTS

28-bar duple-minor longways; moderate.
dance & tune: Thompson. This is believed to have been written by Newport Gardner, African-born resident of Newport.

1-8	All set twice; half right & lefts.
9-16	All set twice; half right & lefts.
17-28	The 1 woman cast off (followed by her partner), dance up between the 2s, dance counterclockwise around the 2 man and return to original places (all in 12 counts); 1s cast off (2s move up); partners turn once around with 2 hands.

BOSCAWEN'S FROLIC

32-bar triple-minor longways; moderate.
dance & tune: Thompson. Admiral Edward Boscawen began the British conquest of French Canada in 1758, thus earning the gratitude of Americans who had been living in fear of a French invasion.

1-8	1s go down the outside for 8 counts, turn and come back.
9-16	1s lead down the middle, cast back up around the 3s into 2nd place, lead up to first place and cast off (2s move up), and end facing first corners.
17-24	1s set to first corners, set to partners (may be best to be improper at this stage), set to second corners and set to partner.
25-32	1s lead out at the sides (lead out between 2 & 3 women, separate and cast in around the ends ; lead out between 2 & 3 men, separate and cast in around ends to pro-gressed places proper).

BOSTON ASSEMBLY

40-bar duple-minor longways; moderate.
dance: Griffiths II, 1794; tune: On the Road to Boston, Pike MS.

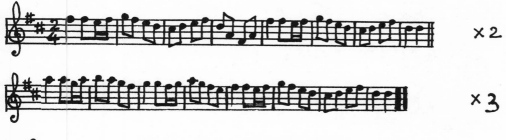

1-8	1s and 2s dance a right-hand star and a left-hand star back.
9-16	Partners allemande right and then allemande left.
17-24	1s go down the middle, come back and cast off (2s moving up).
25-32	1s and 2s circle to the left and circle back to the right.
33-40	1s and 2s dance rights & lefts, four changes, starting with partners facing.

BOSTON'S DELIGHT
40-bar triple-minor longways; moderate.
dance; Weeks MS, 1783; tune: Greenwood MS

1-8	1s cast down the outside for 8 counts and come back (more slowly) straight to pro-gressed places (2s having moved up).
9-16	1s and the couple below circle to the left and circle back to the right.
17-24	1s and 2s dance rights & lefts, four changes, starting with partners facing.
25-32	1s set to first corners, set to partners (may be best to be improper at this stage), set to second corners and set to partner.
33-40	1s lead out at the sides (lead out between 2 & 3 women, separate and cast in around the ends ; lead out between 2 & 3 men, separate and cast in around ends to pro-gressed places proper).

THE BRANDEWINE
32-bar triple-minor longways; moderate;
dance & tune: Cantelo, 1785.

1-8	1 man set twice to 2 woman, but turn 3 woman once around with 2 hands, retur-ning to place afterwards.
9-16	1 woman set twice to 2 man, but turn 3 man once around with 2 hands, returning to place afterwards.
17-24	1s go down the middle, come back and cast off (2s moving up).
25-32	Partners allemande right and then allemande left.

BRITISH SORROW

32-bar triple or duple-minor longways; moderate.
dance: Saltator II, 1807; tune: The World Turn'd Upside Down, trad.

1-8	1s go down the middle, come back and cast off (2s moving up).
9-16	1s dance a right-hand star once around with the couple below and a left-hand star once around with the couple above.
17-24	circle to the left and circle back to the right.
25-32	1s and 2s dance rights & lefts, four changes, starting with partners facing.

THE BUSIE BODY

32-bar duple-minor longways; moderate.
dance & tune: Feuillet/Essex, 1710; this book is known to have been owned by American dance teachers in the 18th century.

1-8	1 man cast off, chased by partner, come in below 2 man and return up the middle, looping into places.
9-16	1 woman cast off, chased by partner, come in below 2 woman and return up the middle, looping into places.
17-24	1s cast off slowly (2s move up); all jump into the center on count 8; partners pattacake; 1s cast up in 4 counts (2s move down).
25-32	Circle to the left for 4 counts; cloverleaf turn single; complete circle; 1s cast in 4 counts (2s move up).

CAMERON'S RANT/CAMERONIAN RANT

32-bar triple-minor longways, possibly a strathspey; moderate.
dance: Griffiths I, 1788; tune: Turner MS.

1-8	1s go down the outside for 8 counts, turn and come back.
9-16	1s go down the middle, come back and cast off (2s moving up).
17-24	1s turn first corners once around with 2 hands, then turn second corners once around with 2 hands.
25-32	Partial poussette: 1 man push and 2 man pull for 4 counts; partners set; return to places with couples reversing direction; partners set.

CAPT. OAKES' WHIM

40-bar triple or duple-minor longways; moderate.
dance & tune: Cantelo, 1785.

1-8	1s go down the outside for 8 counts, turn and come back.
9-16	1s go down the middle, come back and cast off (2s moving up).
17-24	Partners set and overhead allemande by the right; circle once around to the left.
25-32	1s lead down through the couple below, cast back up, lead up through the couple above and cast back down.
33-40	1s and 2s dance rights & lefts, four changes, starting with partners facing.

CHESHIRE ROUNDS
16-bar (triple time) duple-minor longways; moderate.
dance & tune: Playford 11th edition, 1701; tune in Parkman MS.

1-8   Turn single quickly to the left and circle (without hands) to the left, then take hands and circle back to the right; repeat in the opposite directions, starting with a quick turn single to the right.

9-16   1s cross & cast and turn half way around with 2 hands to proper sides; dance rights & lefts.

CHORUS JIG
32-bar triple-minor longways; moderate.
dance: An Elegant Collection . . . by W.D., 1798; tune: Dodd, 1795.

1-8   1s chasser down the outside for 4 counts; rigadoon; chasser back and rigadoon.

9-16   1s go down the middle, come back and cast off (2s moving up).

17-24   1s turn first corners once around with 2 hands, then turn second corners once around with 2 hands.

25-32   1s lead out the men's side for 4 counts and rigadoon, lead back to places and quickly turn once around   with 2 hands.

CITY OF PARIS
24-bar duple-minor longways; moderate.
dance: Moore/Ridgely MS, 1790s; tune: Clark MS.

1-8   Partners change sides in 4 counts; 1s chasser down the middle 4 small steps while 2s chasser up the outside, thus changing places; Partners change sides in 4 counts; repeat chasser back to places, the 1s slipping up the outside.

9-16   1s go down the middle, come back and cast off (2s moving up).

17-24   1s and 2s dance rights & lefts, four changes, starting with partners facing.

CITY OF WASHINGTON
24-bar duple-minor longways; easy.
dance & tune: Dodd, 1795.

1-8   Partners set twice and turn once and a half around by the right.

9-16   Partners set twice and turn once and a half around by the left.

17-24   1s go down the middle, come back and cast off (2s moving up).

COLUMBIA
16-bar triple or duple-minor longways; easy.
dance & tune: Massachusetts Magazine, 1790.

1-8   1s turn by the right half way and cast off improper, turn by the left half way and cast again below the next couple, proper.

9-16   1s lead up to the top and cast off, then lead through the couple below and cast back up to progressed places.

CONSTANCY

32-bar duple-minor longways; moderate.
dance: Griffiths I, 1788; tune: Beck MS.

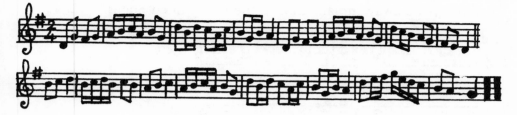

1-8	1s and 2s dance a right-hand star and a left-hand star back.
9-16	1s go down the middle, come back and cast off (2s moving up).
17-24	Partners set twice and turn once around with 2 hands.
25-32	1s and 2s dance rights & lefts, four changes, starting with partners facing.

CONSTITUTION OF AMERICA

32-bar duple-minor longways; moderate.
dance: Moore/Ridgely MS, 1790s; tune: American ca.1800.

1-8	1s set twice to the 2 woman, then all 3 circle once around to the left.
9-16	1s set twice to the 2 man, then all 3 circle once around to the left.
17-24	1s go down the middle, come back and cast off (2s moving up).
25-32	1s and 2s dance rights & lefts, four changes, starting with partners facing.

THE CORNPLANTER

32-bar triple-minor longways; moderate.
dance: Griffiths II, 1794; tune: Carroll MS; Cornplanter was an important Seneca Chief who incurred unpopularity with many Indians for giving away Indian lands to the new United States.

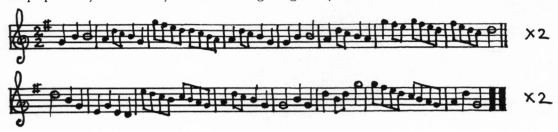

1-8	1s go down the middle, come back and cast off (2s moving up).
9-16	Partners take left hands and set twice to first corners, then take right hands and set twice to second corners.
17-24	1s and the couple below circle to the left and circle back to the right.
25-32	1s and 2s dance rights & lefts, four changes, starting with partners facing.

CORSINO/CASINO

32-bar duple-minor longways; moderate.
dance: Champlin MS, 1781; tune: Hawkins MS, etc.; the Champlin MS was written by Peggy Champlin after she had danced with George Washington in Newport in 1781; it has been lost, but parts of it were published by a descendant, George Champlin Mason in 1884.

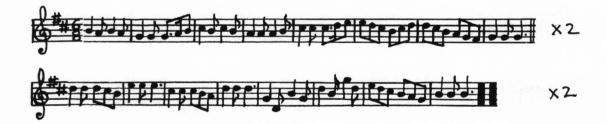

1-8	Partners set twice, and change sides in 8 counts
9-16	Partners set twice and change back again.
17-24	Partners allemande right; 1s cast off in 8 counts (2s move up on 5–8).
25-32	1s and 2s dance rights & lefts, four changes, starting with partners facing.

DEVIL'S DREAM/DEVIL AMONG THE TAILORS

32-bar duple-minor longways; moderate.
dance: Leominster book, 1799; tune: Carroll MS.

1-8	1s and 2s dance a right-hand star and a left-hand star back.
9-16	1s go down the outside for 8 counts, turn and come back.
17-24	1s go down the middle, come back and cast off (2s moving up).
25-32	1s and 2s dance rights & lefts, four changes, starting with partners facing.

DIBDIN'S FANCY

28-bar duple-minor longways; moderate.
dance & tune: Young's Vocal and Instrumental Musical Miscellany, 1793. Charles Dibdin (1745–1814) was one of Britain's best songwriters and a composer of many operettas.

1-8	Second corners set twice and turn once around with 2 hands.
9-16	First corners set twice and turn once around with 2 hands.
17-24	1s go down the middle, come back and cast off (2s moving up).
25-28	partners turn once around with 2 hands.

THE DILIGENT
36-bar duple-minor longways in two parts; moderate-difficult.
dance & tune: Feuillet/Essex, 1710.

PART I
1-8
1 woman dances down through the 2s and clockwise around the 2 man to stand in the middle just above the 2s facing down, while the 1 man crosses over and casts down to below the 2s, where he stands facing up; then each 2 dances counterclockwise around the 1 one the left and returns to places.
9-18
1s turn once and a quarter around with 2 hands to fall into progressed places proper (2s move up); 2s turn once around with 2 hands.

PART II
1-8
In 8 counts for each change, 1s cross over with a belly-to-belly change, then neighbors do likewise.
9-18
Circle once around to the left and fall back; 1s dance half a figure-8 up through the 2s.

DON FISCO
32-bar duple-minor longways; moderate.
dance: Muzzey MS, 1795; tune: Greenwood MS.

1-8	1 & 2 women take near hands, set twice, lead between partners and cast separately back to places.
9-16	1 & 2 men do likewise.
17-24	1s go down the middle, come back and cast off (2s moving up).
25-32	1s and 2s dance rights & lefts, four changes, starting with partners facing.

THE DONOP/LADY MARY MURRAY'S FANTAISIE
24-bar duple-minor longways; moderate.
dance & tune: Cantelo, 1785; Carl Emil Kurt von Donop was a German mercenary colonel fighting for the British in New Jersey, where he was killed in 1777.

1-8	Partners set and change sides, set and change back again.
9-16	1s go down the middle, come back and cast off (2s moving up).
17-24	Partners allemande right half way, set, allemande left back and set.

THE DUCHESS OF ATHOL'S STRATHSPEY
24-bar duple-minor longways strathspey; moderate.
dance & tune: Frobischer MS, 1793. The famous Scottish fiddler, Neil Gow, worked for the Athol family and may have written this dance and tune.

1-8	Partners strathspey set, change places, strathspey set and change back (take small steps and loop around so as to fill the time available for the changing of places).
9-16	1s go down the middle, come back and cast off (2s moving up).
17-24	1s and 2s dance rights & lefts, four changes, starting with partners facing.

THE DUCHESS OF YORK'S FANCY
32-bar triple or duple-minor longways; moderate.
dance & tune: Frobischer MS, 1793.

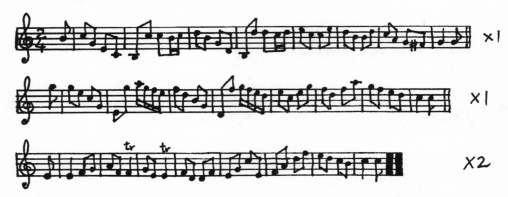

1-8	1s and 2s dance a right-hand star and a left-hand star back.
9-16	1s go down the middle, come back and cast off (2s moving up).
17-24	Partners allemande right; circle once around with the couple below.
25-32	1s and 2s dance rights & lefts, four changes, starting with partners facing.

THE DUKE OF KENT'S WALTZ
32-bar triple or duple-minor longways in triple time; moderate-easy.
dance & tune: anonymous MS in British Museum; Prince Edward Augustus (1767–1820), a younger son of George III, was created Duke of Kent in 1799, and the dance was presumably written at that time. Edward's daughter became Queen Victoria in 1837. Edward was stationed with the British military in Canada and the Caribbean 1791–1799, and many balls were held in his honor.

1-8	1s and 2s dance a right-hand star and a left-hand star back.
9-16	1s take both hands and chasser 2 slow steps down the middle and 2 steps back; cast off (2s move up).
17-24	Allemandes, thus: partners take right hands, balance forward, balance back and change places with right overhead allemande; repeat to places by the left.
25-32	All turn the person diagonally on the right once around by the right; partners turn once around by the left.

THE DUKE OF YORK'S FANCY

24-bar duple-minor longways; moderate-easy.
dance & tune: Frobischer MS, 1793.

1-8	1s go down the outside for 8 counts, turn and come back.
9-16	1s cross & cast (2s move up) and turn one and a half times around with 2 hands to proper sides.
17-24	1s and 2s dance rights & lefts, four changes, starting with partners facing.

DURANG'S HORNPIPE

24-bar duple-minor longways; moderate.
dance: Leominster book, 1799; tune: Carroll MS; John Durang was the first important American-born solo dance performer (mostly hornpipes). While he was performing in New York in 1785 he met a German composer called Hoffmeister (only 3 feet tall!), who wrote this tune for him.

1-8	1s go down the outside for 8 counts, turn and come back.
9-16	1s go down the middle, come back and cast off (2s moving up).
17-24	1s and 2s dance rights & lefts, four changes, starting with partners facing.

L'ESCAPADE
24-bar duple-minor longways; moderate.
dance & tune: Cantelo, 1785.

1-8	All set, rigadoon and circle (chasser step) to the left for 4 counts; repeat back to the right.
9-16	1s go down the middle, come back and cast off (2s moving up).
17-24	Partners allemande right and then allemande left.

THE FAIR AMERICAN
24-bar duple-minor longways; moderate.
dance: Moore/Ridgely MS, 1790s; tune: Cary MS; the title is the name of a privateer ship that fought in the War of Independence.

1-8	1s take hands in a ring with the 2 woman and set twice; 1s take hands in a ring with the 2 man and set twice.
9-16	1s go down the middle, come back and cast off (2s moving up).
17-24	1s and 2s dance rights & lefts, four changes, starting with partners facing.

THE FAIR EMIGRANT/MRS. DAWSON'S DELIGHT
32-bar duple-minor longways; moderate.
dance & tune: Cantelo, 1785, written by Colonel Cosmo Gordon.

THE FAIR EMIGRANT/MRS. DAWSON'S DELIGHT

1-8   Second corners set and turn once around quickly in 4 counts; first corners do likewise.

9-16   1s chasser down the middle 4 steps, rigadoon, dance back up only to progressed places, turning once around with 2 hands as they go (2s having moved up).

17-24   Partners set and turn half way around by the right; set and turn half way around by the left, to places.

25-32   Take hands in a ring, set twice and circle (chasser step) once around to the right.

THE FAITHFUL SHEPHERD

24-bar duple-minor longways; moderate.
dance & tune: Thompson, 1769; this dance, which was presumably devised in 1734, the year Handel's opera Il Pastor Fido was revived, is listed as one of three dances danced at the Turtle Frolic at Newport in 1752, many years before it was published, and was mentioned in Peggy Champlin's MS of 1781.

1-8   1s and 2s dance a right-hand star and a left-hand star back.

9-16   1s cross & cast (2s move up) and turn one and a half times around with 2 hands to proper sides.

17-24   1s and 2s dance rights & lefts, four changes, starting with partners facing.

THE FANTOCINI

32-bar triple or duple-minor longways; moderate.
dance: Griffiths I, 1788; tune: Thompson III.

1-8   Partners set and change sides, set and change back again.

9-16   1s go down the middle, come back and cast off (2s moving up).

17-24   1s and the couple below dance a right-hand star and a left-hand star back.

25-32   Partners allemande right and then allemande left.

THE FEMALE SAILOR
32-bar duple-minor longways; moderate-easy.
dance & tune: Feuillet/Essex, 1710; alternate tune, Peirce MS.

alternate tune: La Matelotte Anglaise

1-8	1s lead up through the 2s above, cast back, lead down through the 2s below and cast back.
9-16	1s dance half a figure-8 down through the couple below; partners turn once around by the **right**, ending with the 1s facing down and the 2s facing up.
17-24	Neighbors dos-à-dos, then turn once around with 2 hands.
25-32	1s dos a dos (actually, 2s can do it as well); then 1s turn half way around with 2 hands and cast off (2s move up).

THE FIRST ASSEMBLY
48-bar triple or duple-minor longways; moderate.
dance & tune: Philadelphia MS, 1783.

1-8	Partners set then quick rights & lefts (2 counts per side) for 2 changes; set again and complete the rights & lefts.
9-16	1s and 2s dance a right-hand star and a left-hand star back.
17-24	1s go down the middle, come back and cast off (2s moving up).
25-32	1s and 2s dance rights & lefts, four changes, starting with partners facing.
33-40	Partners set twice; 1s lead up through the 2s above and cast back.
41-48	Partners set twice; 1s lead down through the couple below and cast back.

THE FIRST OF MAY
24-bar duple-minor longways; moderate.
dance: Griffiths I, 1788; tune: Turner MS.

1-8	Neighbors take 2 hands and chasser out 4 steps, balancer, chasser back again and balancer.
9-16	1s go down the middle, come back and cast off (2s moving up).
17-24	Men chasser 4 small steps towards partner and chasser back to places; then women do likewise.

THE FOUR SEASONS
40-bar triple-minor longways; moderate.
dance: Moore/Ridgely MS, 1790s; tune: Carroll MS.

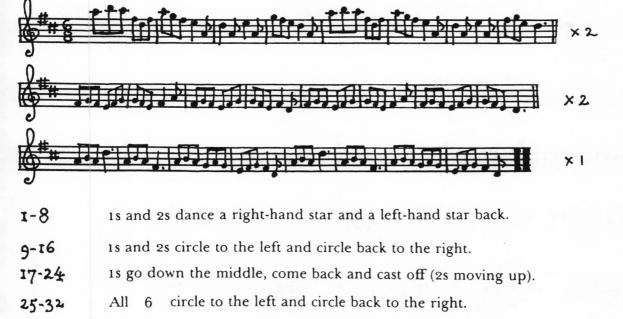

1-8	1s and 2s dance a right-hand star and a left-hand star back.
9-16	1s and 2s circle to the left and circle back to the right.
17-24	1s go down the middle, come back and cast off (2s moving up).
25-32	All 6 circle to the left and circle back to the right.
33-40	1s and 2s dance rights & lefts, four changes, starting with partners facing.

THE FREEMASON'S JIG
64-bar triple-minor longways; moderate.
dance & tune: Thompson ; tune in Murphey MS, 1790.

×2 (+2)

×2 (+2)

1-8	The 3 men take hands and the third man lead them counterclockwise around the 3 women.
9-16	The 3 women take hands and the third woman lead them clockwise around the 3 men.
17-24	1s go down the middle, come back and cast off (2s moving up).
25-32	1s turn once around by the right, then three-quarters around by the left, ending with the man between the 2s facing down and the woman between the 3s facing up.
33-40	Lines of three step to the right and honor, step to the left and honor; 1s turn three-quarters around with 2 hands to end proper in middle places.
41-48	New lines of 3 step to the right and honor, step to the left and honor; partners turn once around with 2 hands.
49-56	Lines fall back a double and come forward; partners turn once and a half around with 2 hands.
57-64	Lines fall back a double and come forward; partners turn once and a half around with 2 hands.

GENERAL ABERCROMBIE'S REEL/THE LIGHT BOB
32-bar triple-minor longways; moderate.
dance & tune: Cantelo, 1785; written by Colonel Cosmo Gordon.

1-8	1s chasser down the outside for 4 counts; rigadoon; chasser back and rigadoon.
9-16	1s go down the middle, come back and cast off (2s moving up).
17-24	1s set to first corners and turn them once around with 2 hands in 4 counts, then set to and turn second corners.
25-32	1s lead out at the sides (lead out between 2 & 3 women, separate and cast in around the ends ; lead out between 2 & 3 men, separate and cast in around ends to progressed places proper).

GODDESSES

96-bar four-couple longways set; difficult.
dance & tune: Playford I, 1651; tune in Parkman MS, 1720.

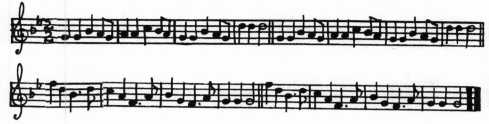

FIRST VERSE: Partners take near hands, lead up a double and fall back again, twice.

CHORUS: 1s cast off, followed by the others, and invert the set (skipping step), then cast back to places, followed by the others.

SECOND VERSE: Men take hands and 1 man lead the line across the top of the set and down behind the women's line while the women do likewise inside the men's loop; the sets are now inverted and improper; repeat to places, the 4 man and 4 woman leading (skipping step).

THIRD VERSE: With the 2s and 3s falling back, each line forms a separate circle; men slip 8 counts to the left and back to the right, while women slip right and back to the left.

FOURTH VERSE: The two lines join at the ends to form a large circle; slip left for 8 counts and back to the right.

FIFTH VERSE: 1s & 3s face down while 2s & 4s face up; each separate line dances a straight hey for four, starting by passing right shoulders.

SIXTH VERSE: All face as in the fifth verse, but dance a circular hey all around the set.

NOTE: If it is desired to lengthen the dance, it is appropriate to add two extra verses: Partners side to right shoulders and then to left shoulders, between verses 3 & 4; and Partners arm right and arm left, between verses 5 & 6.

THE GORDIAN KNOT

16-bar duple-minor improper longways, or foursome Scots reel; moderate.
dance: Saltator I   1802; tune: Bride, ca.1782.

1-8   1s (improper) face down and 2s face up; neighbors set twice and turn once around (those in men's line   by the right and those in the women's line by the left).

9-16   Double figure-8 hey or reel ending in progressed places (2s start up the outside while 1s cross going down the middle; then 1s do what 2s did and vice versa; repeat to places, and a little further to   progress).

GRIFFITHS' FANCY

(24 or) 32-bar triple or duple-minor longways; moderate.
dance: Griffiths I, 1788; tune: Mrs. Griffiths' Hornpipe, Ash Ms, 1818.

1-8	1s and 2s dance a right-hand star and a left-hand star back.
9-16	1s cross & cast (2s move up), then set and turn half way with 2 hands to end proper.
17-24	1s circle to the left and back to the right with the couple below.
25-32	1s and 2s dance rights & lefts, four changes, starting with partners facing.

GRIFFITHS' WHIM

32-bar triple or duple-minor longways; moderate.
dance: Griffiths I, 1788; tune: Turner MS.

1-8	1s turn half way around by the right and set, then lead down through the 2s and cast back up, improper.
9-16	2s turn half way around by the right and set, then lead up through the 1s and cast back down improper.
17-24	Take hands on the sides and set twice; right hand star once around.
25-32	Take hands on the sides and set twice; 1s and 2s dance rights & lefts half way.

THE GROVES
32-bar duple-minor longways; moderate.
dance: Griffiths I, 1788; tune: Carroll Ms.

I-8	1s and 2s dance a right-hand star and a left-hand star back.
9-16	1s go down the middle, come back and cast off (2s moving up).
17-24	1s and 2s circle to the left and circle back to the right.
25-32	1s and 2s dance rights & lefts, four changes, starting with partners facing.

GUARDIAN ANGELS
48-bar triple-minor longways; moderate-difficult.
dance & tune: Thompson, 1780; tune found in numerous early American collections.

I-8	Partners set; 1s cast down (2s move up); partners set; 1s cast down again (3s move up).
9-16	Partners set; 1s cast up one place (3s move down); partners set; 1s cast up (2s move down).
17-24	1s cross & cast (2s move up); 1s cross & cast again (3s move up).
25-32	1s cross & cast up one place (3s move down); 1s cross & cast up (2s move down).
33-40	1 man dance a right-hand star with the 3s half way around while the 1 woman does likewise with the 2s for 4 counts; all six circle to the left half way around in 4 counts; 1 man dance a left-hand star half way around with the 2s while the 1 woman does likewise with the 3s for 4 counts; all six circle back to the right for 4 counts; 1s should end proper and in middle places.
41-48	1 man dance a straight hey for 3 with the 3s for 8 counts while the 1 woman does likewise with the 2s; 1s switch ends and hey again, ending in middle places proper.

HAMBLETON'S ROUND-O

16-bar triple-minor longways in triple time; moderate-difficult.

dance & tune: Playford vol.II, known to have been owned in America in the 18th century.

1-8   1s cast off (2s move up); 1 man hey with the 3s while 1 woman hey with the 2s; 1s turn half way around with 2 hands to end proper and progressed.

9-16   1 woman & 2 man change places quickly by right shoulders, then other corners likewise; 1s & 2s circle half way around to the left and turn single cloverleaf; 1s & 2s dance 4 changes of a circular hey, 3 counts per side.

THE HAMILTONIAN/LADY AMELIA MURRAY'S CHOICE

48-bar triple or duple-minor longways; moderate.

dance & tune: Cantelo, 1785, written by Colonel Cosmo Gordon.

Second corners set twice and turn once around with 2 hands.

First corners set twice and turn once around with 2 hands.

1s go down the middle, come back and cast off (2s moving up).

Partners set twice and allemande right.

Partners set twice; 1s circle once around to the right with the couple below.

1s and 2s dance rights & lefts, four changes, starting with partners facing.

HANDEL'S MARCH COUNTRY DANCE

32-bar triple-minor longways; moderate.
dance: Muzzey MS, 1795; tune: Pike MS; musicologists specializing in Handel say that the tune is not found among Handel's doumented works, which of course does not necessarily mean that he did not write it.

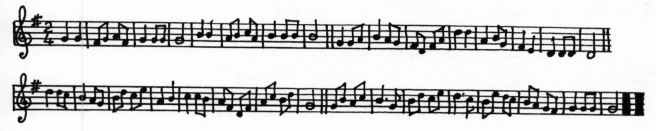

1-8	1s cross & cast (2s move up) and turn one and a half times around with 2 hands to proper sides.
9-16	1s dance a figure-8 up through the 2s.
17-24	1 woman circle with the 2s around to the left and back to the right, while 1 man does likewise with the 3s.
25-32	1s and 2s dance rights & lefts, four changes, starting with partners facing.

HASTE TO THE WEDDING

32-bar duple-minor improper longways; easy.
dance: traditional; tune: from the operetta The Elopement, 1767. This tune, known variously as Haste to the Wedding, Come Haste, Rural Felicity, and even The Rules of Felicity, has had dozens of sets of dance directions paired with it; the set chosen here seems to fit the music best of them all. The tune appeared in America first in Aaron Thompson MS, 1777.

1-8	1s and 2s dance a right-hand star and a left-hand star back.
9-16	1s and 2s circle to the left and circle back to the right.
17-24	Partners dos a dos, clap, clap, and turn once around with 2 hands.
25-32	Neighbors dos a dos, clap, clap, and turn half way around with 2 hands.

91

HAYMAKING/THE HAYMAKER'S
32-bar duple-minor longways; moderate.
dance & tune: Neal, 1726; mentioned in Champlin MS, 1781.

x2

x2

1-8	1 man cast down below 2 man while 2 woman cast up above 1 woman, and turn with left hands back to places.
9-16	2 man cast up above 1 man while 1 woman cast down below 2 woman, and turn with right hands back to places.
17-24	Take hands with neighbor, fall back a double and set; 1s, turning once around with 2 hands, dance down the middle to progressed place while the 2s cast up.
25-32	Right-hand star half way around and fall back; 2 changes of rights & lefts.

THE HEREDITARY PRINCE
32-bar triple-minor longways; moderate.
dance & tune: Cantelo, 1785.

1-8	Right-hand star once around and circle back to the right.
9-16	1s go down the middle, come back and cast off (2s moving up).
17-24	1s turn once around by the left, then turn first corner by the right.
25-32	1s turn once around by the left, then turn second corner by the right.

HEY HO FOR MY HONEY

24-bar duple-minor longways; moderate.

dance: A New Academy, 1795; tune: Playford 3rd edition supplement, 1657. This dance is one of those cases where Playford made a serious typographical error, repeating himself by accident, so that the dance makes little sense; it was nevertheless reprinted through many editions! A New Academy corrected all but one word of the error, but that reduced the dance to 16 bars, whereas Playford's tune was 24 bars long.

1-8
1s cast off, 1 man going below the 2 man and up the middle to top place and the 1 woman going below the 2 woman to stand between the 2s facing up; the 1 man alone dances up a double with the line of three abreast following behind him; the 1 man faces down, and all set.

9-16
[repeat — 1 woman do what the 1 man did.]

17-24
The 1s cross by right shoulders and proceed thus: 1 man dances clockwise around the 2 woman and ends in 1 woman's place while the 1 woman dances counterclockwise around the 2 man to end in 1 man's place; 1s set, cast off (2s moving up) and cross back to proper sides.

HOBSON'S CHOICE

40-bar triple or duple-minor longways; moderate.

dance & tune: Frobischer MS, 1793. Thomas Hobson (died 1631), an English liveryman, ordered his customers to take the next available horse rather than give them a choice.

1-8   1s and 2s set twice; half right & lefts.

9-16   1s and 2s set twice; half right & lefts.

17-24   1s dance down the middle for 6 counts and come back up to progressed places in 2 counts (2s having moved up); partners allemande right.

25-32   1s and the couple below circle to the left and circle back to the right.

33-40   1s and 2s dance rights & lefts, four changes, starting with partners facing.

93

HOW IMPERFECT IS EXPRESSION

32-bar triple-minor longways; moderate.
dance & tune: Cantelo, 1785, written by Captain Oakes.

1-8	1s and 2s dance a right-hand star and a left-hand star back.
9-16	1s and 2s circle to the left and circle back to the right.
17-24	1s lead down the middle and cast back up around 3s to 2nd place (2s move up); 3s lead up the middle and cast back down around 2s all the way to third place.
25-32	Partners set, rigadoon and allemande right.

HOWE'S ARMY

16-bar duple-minor longways; moderate.
dance & tune: Fishar, 1780. General Sir William Howe (pronounced Ho) was reluctantly in command of all British land forces in America 1775–1778. He and his brother, Vice Admiral Richard Lord Howe, both sympathized with Americans and thus pressed the war with less vigor than that needed to win.

1-8

First corners take crossed hands, turn half way around to change places, then raise the hands and return to places in overhead allemande position; then second corners do likewise.

9-16

2s make an arch so 1s can cast off and come back up through the arch; then 1s make an arch so 2s can lead up through the arch, cast off and lead up again quickly (the 1s casting off).

THE HUMOUR OF BOSTON
32-bar triple or duple-minor longways; easy.
dance: Griffiths II, 1794; tune: Carroll MS.

1-8	1s go down the outside for 8 counts, turn and come back.
9-16	1s and 2s circle to the left and circle back to the right.
17-24	1s go down the middle, come back and cast off (2s moving up).
25-32	All 3 couples circle once around to the left and circle back to the right.

IANTHA
42-bar triple-minor longways; moderate.
dance & tune: Playford 13th edition, 1706; tune in Parkman MS, 1720.

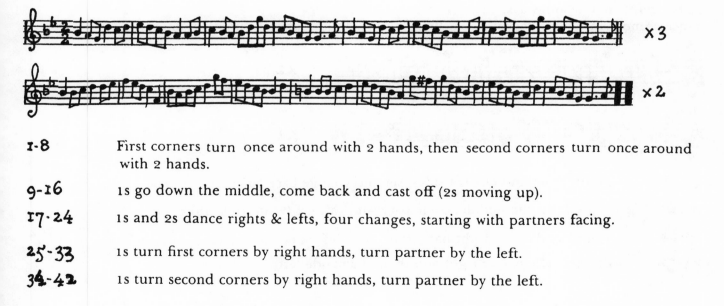

1-8	First corners turn once around with 2 hands, then second corners turn once around with 2 hands.
9-16	1s go down the middle, come back and cast off (2s moving up).
17-24	1s and 2s dance rights & lefts, four changes, starting with partners facing.
25-33	1s turn first corners by right hands, turn partner by the left.
34-42	1s turn second corners by right hands, turn partner by the left.

IN THE FIELDS IN FROST & SNOW

24-bar duple-minor longways; moderate-easy.
dance & tune: Playford vol.II; the tune was written by Draghi, a London relative of the famous Pergolesi.

1-8   1s turn half way around by the right and cast off (2s move up), turn half way around by the left and   cast back up (2s move down).

9-16   Taking hands with neighbor, all dance forward a double and fall back a double; turn single and circle   half way around to the left.

17-24   1 man & 2 woman change places by right shoulders, then other corners the same; 1s set and cast off   (2s move up).

THE INDIAN PRINCESS

32-bar duple-minor longways; easy.
dance: American Ladies Pocket Book, Philadelphia, 1796; dance & tune: Thompson, 1796.

1-8   Partners set and change sides, set and change back again.

9-16   1s go down the middle, come back and cast off (2s moving up).

17-24   1s and 2s dance a right-hand star and a left-hand star back.

25-32   Partners allemande right and then allemande left.

THE INDIAN QUEEN

32-bar duple-minor longways; moderate-easy.

dance & tune: Playford 9th edition, 1695. It is just possible that Purcell wrote the music for this dance, which is named after Dryden's historically inaccurate play about pre-Columbian Indians of Mexico, for which Purcell wrote the incidental music, the last music he ever wrote.

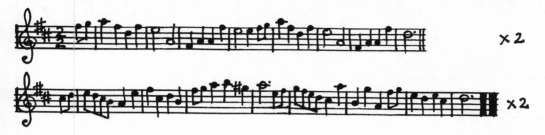

1-8	First corners set, turn single and turn once around with 2 hands.
9-16	Second corners do likewise.
17-24	1s and 2s dance a right-hand star and a left-hand star back.
25-32	Partners dos a dos, then three changes of a circular hey (starting with partners facing) to progressed places.

IRISH LAMENTATION

48-bar duple-minor longways in triple time; moderate.

dance & tune: Walsh Third Book; tune in Wilkes Allen MS. The directions given here are those adapted for modern dancers who do not do the minuet step, so here are the original directions: First man dances the Minuet Step to the 2d.wo. and turns her—the 2d.man the same to the 1st wo. = the 1st Cu.cast down and up again then cross over and half figure then right hand and left quite round and turn your partner.

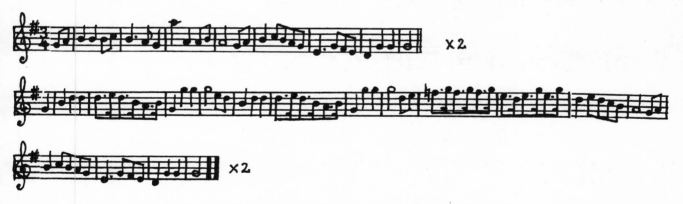

1-8	Take hands in a ring and balancer twice (some people like to start to the left first); first corners turn once around with 2 hands.
9-16	Repeat, with second corners turning.
17-32	Partners lead up for 3 counts and 1s (perhaps assisted by 2s) **cast down**; partners lead down for 3 counts and 1s (perhaps assisted) cast back up; 1s cross & cast (2s move up) and dance a half figure-8 up through the 2s.
33-48	Rights & lefts, 6 counts per side, then a clockwise whole poussette.

THE ISLE OF SKYE
24-bar duple-minor longways; moderate-easy.
dance: Griffiths I, 1788; tune: Atholl Collection; also found in Frobischer MS, 1793.

1-8	1s go down the outside for 8 counts, turn and come back.
9-16	1s go down the middle, come back and cast off (2s moving up).
17-24	Men face down and women face up; all chasser 4 steps across the set (partners passing face to face); rigadoon, chasser back and rigadoon.

JACK'S ALIVE/JACK'S DELIGHT
24-bar duple-minor improper longways; moderate.
dance: Weeks MS, 1783; tune: Greenwood MS.

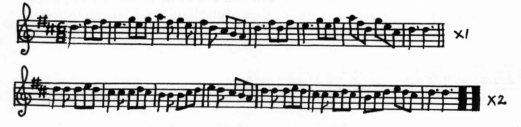

1-8	1s improper, all face out; neighbors lead out a double, set, lead back and set again.
9-16	1s cross & cast (2s move up) and turn one and a half times around with 2 hands to proper sides.
17-24	1s and 2s dance rights & lefts, four changes, starting with partners facing.

JACKSON'S MORNING [or MOURNING] BRUSH

32-bar duple-minor longways; easy.
dance: Moore/Ridgely MS, 1790s; tune: Aaron Thompson MS, 1777.

1-8	1s go down the outside for 8 counts, turn and come back.
9-16	1s and 2s dance a right-hand star and a left-hand star back.
17-24	1s go down the middle, come back and cast off (2s moving up).
25-32	1s and 2s circle to the left and circle back to the right.

JAMAICA

16 or 32-bar duple-minor longways in 2 parts; moderate-easy.
Playford 4th edition, 1670 (not long after the British conquest of Jamaica from Spain).

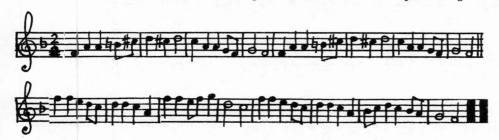

PART I

1-8

1s take right hand in left hand then add left hand in left hand and change places, ending facing down; neighbors repeat what 1s did and end facing in, still holding crossed hands.

9-16

Still holding crossed hands, fall back a double and come forward a double; 1s dance half a figure-8 up through the 2s.

PART II

1-8

First corners turn once around with 2 hands; second corners turn once around with 2 hands.

9-16

Neighbors (skipping step) turn once and a half around with 2 hands; then partners (walking step) turn once around with two hands.

JEFFERSON & LIBERTY

32-bar duple-minor longways; moderate.
dance: Saltator II, 1807; tune: Shattuck MS, 18th c.

1-8	1s go down the outside for 8 counts, turn and come back.
9-16	1s go down the middle, come back and cast off (2s moving up).
17-24	1s and 2s circle to the left and circle back to the right.
25-32	1s and 2s dance rights & lefts, four changes, starting with partners facing.

LADY BUCKLEY'S [sic BERKELEY'S] WHIM

32 or 40-bar triple-minor longways; moderate.
dance: Griffiths I, 1788; tune: Johnson, 1751.

1-8	1s go down the outside for 8 counts, turn and come back.
9-16	1s go down the middle, come back and cast off (2s moving up).
17-24	End the cast-off with 1 woman facing up between the 3s and 1 man facing down between the 2s; all set; 1s turn three-quarters around with 2 hands to end in second place proper; all set.
[suggest omit]	[All 3 couples circle to the left and circle back to the right.]
25-32	1s and 2s dance rights & lefts, four changes, starting with partners facing.

LADY GEORGE MURRAY'S REEL
32-bar triple-minor longways; moderate.
dance & tune: Cantelo, 1785, written by Colonel Cosmo Gordon.

1-8	1s and 2s dance a right-hand star and a left-hand star back.
9-16	1s go down the middle, come back and cast off (2s moving up).
17-24	1s set to first corners and turn them once around with 2 hands in 4 counts, then set to and turn second corners.
25-32	1s lead out at the sides (lead out between 2 & 3 women, separate and cast in around the ends ; lead out between 2 & 3 men, separate and cast in around ends to progressed places proper).

LADY HARRIOT HOPE'S REEL
32-bar triple-minor longways; moderate.
dance & tune: Frobischer MS, 1793.

1-8	1s go down the outside for 8 counts, turn and come back.
9-16	1s go down the middle, come back and cast off (2s moving up).
17-24	1s turn first corners once around with 2 hands, then turn second corners once around with 2 hands.
25-32	1s and 2s dance rights & lefts, four changes, starting with partners facing.

M. LAFAYETTE

32-bar triple-minor longways; moderate.
dance: Griffiths I, 1788; tune: Turner MS.

1-8	1s dance down and out between the 2 & 3 people on the improper side and come in below the 3s; take hands along the lines and set; 1s return to the top by going up the middle and out between the 2 & 3 people on the proper side.
9-16	1s and 2s circle to the left and circle back to the right.
17-24	1s go down the middle, come back and cast off (2s moving up).
25-32	All six circle around to the left for 8 counts (chasser step?) and back to the right.

LAUREL HILL

32-bar triple-minor longways; moderate-difficult.
dance & tune: Cantelo, 1785.

1-8	1 man circle once around with the 2 & 3 women; then 1 woman circle once around with the 2 & 3 men.
9-16	1s go down the middle, come back and cast off (2s moving up).
17-24	1s & 3s balancer, rigadoon and circle once around to the left.
25-32	1s & 2s balancer, rigadoon and fast rights & lefts (2 counts per side).

THE LEE [LEA] RIGG[S]
32-bar duple-minor longways strathspey; moderate-easy.
dance: 18th-century Scottish MS; tune: Caledonian PC, 1760, and Murphey MS, 1790.

1-8	All turning single to the right dance 1/8 of the way around counterclockwise to form a diamond; strathspey set; in the next turn single, move 1/4 of the way around to the next point of the diamond; strathspey set.
9-16	Continue turning single and setting two more times; during the last setting, the 2s should make certain to move out of the way of the 1s so they can come down the middle in the next phrase.
17-24	1s go down the middle, come back and cast off (2s moving up).
25-32	1s and 2s dance a right-hand star and a left-hand star back.

LIBERTY
32-bar triple-minor longways; moderate.
dance & tune: [American] published by Preston, 1786; Robert Steele, drummer boy at the battle of Bunker Hill in 1775, wrote that this tune (under the name of Welcome Here Again) was very popular with the Americans.

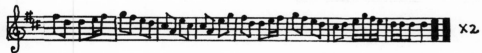

1-16	Three women take hands and dance counterclockwise around the men, the 1 woman leading; then the three men do likewise, clockwise around the women.
17-24	1s go down the middle, come back and cast off (2s moving up).
25-32	1s and 2s dance rights & lefts, four changes, starting with partners facing.

103

LILLI BURLERO
24-bar duple-minor longways; moderate-easy.

dance & tune: Playford 8th edition, 1690, tune attributed to Henry Purcell. Typographical errors in Playford prompted Sharp to invent the unusual figure of a backwards change in a 5-change hey, but the original dance had no such figure, as it was faithfully set forth over a century later in A New Academy, Worcester, MA, 1795.

 x1

 x2

1-8   1s lead down through the 2s and cast back up to places; then 2s lead up through the 1s and cast back to places.

9-16   First corners change places by right shoulders; second corners do likewise; circle to the left half way around and turn single.

17-24   Partners (the book actually says "neighbors", but it works better with partners) dos à dos; three changes of rights & lefts (2 counts for the first 2 changes and 4 counts for the third).

LORD ALBEMARLE'S DELIGHT
24-bar duple-minor longways; moderate.

dance & tune: Johnson, 1751; Lord Albemarle was one of the Proprietors of the two Carolina colonies.

 x2 x4

1-8   1s set to first corners and turn them once around with 2 hands in 4 counts, then set to and turn second corners.

9-16   1s cross by right shoulders, dance below the 2s, cross again by right shoulders and dance back up to places.

17-24   1s chasser down the middle 4 steps, dance back up, set and cast off (2s move up).

LORD ANSON FOR EVER

32-bar triple or duple-minor longways; moderate-difficult.
dance & tune: Johnson. Admiral George Anson made a complete success of his "impossible" mission and brought back to England enormous treasure captured from the Spanish on his voyage around the world in the 1740s. One of his many rewards was a grant of land in Charleston, SC, now a suburb called Ansonborough.

1-8   1s set to first corners and turn them once around with 2 hands in 4 counts, then set to and turn second corners.

9-16   1s cast off and turn in 4 counts once around by the right; cast off below the next couple and turn once around by the left.

17-24   1s dance rights & lefts with the couple above (2 counts per side), then circle once around to the left.

25-32   1s lead up to the top, set to each other and cast off.

LORD BATH'S GATE

24-bar triple or duple-minor longways; moderate.
dance & tune: Thompson III; the dance directions were in the Champlin MS, 1781.

1-8   1s and 2s dance a right-hand star and a left-hand star back.

9-16   1s cast off in 4 counts (2s move up immediately) and allemande right in 4 counts (probably overhead); 1s lead down through the couple below and cast back up to progressed places.

17-24   1s set, lead up through the couple above, cast off and set.

LORD BYRON'S JIG [MY LORD BYRON'S MAGGOT]

28-bar duple-minor longways; moderate.
dance & tune: Playford 11th edition, 1701; tune in Parkman MS, 1720.

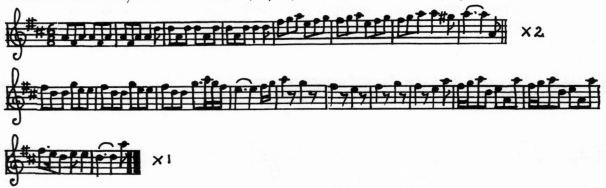

1-8   First corners set twice (first moving towards the man, then moving back to the woman) and turn once around with 2 hands.

9-16   Second corners do likewise.

17-28   The two men take near hands and lead between the two women, separate and cast back to places; partners pattacake twice; 1s cast in 8 counts (2s moving up on 5–8).

[LORD] HOWE'S FLEET

16-bar duple-minor longways; moderate.
dance & tune: Fishar, 1780. Vice Admiral Richard Lord Howe commanded the British naval operations in America in the first years of the War of Independence, and since he liked Americans he failed to prosecute the war with enough vigor to win a quick victory. Sailors fondly called him "Black Dick," because of his dark, weatherbeaten face. He won a smashing victory against the revolutionary French in 1794.

1-8

1s cross hands, chasser down the middle for 4 counts and chasser back; 1s cross over and cast off (2s moving up) and turn half way around with 2 hands.

9-16

1s cross hands, chasser up the middle for only 2 counts, chasser back and cast up above the 2s (2s move down); 2 changes of quick rights & lefts (2 counts a side); partners cross to proper sides.

LORD HOWE'S JIG

32-bar triple-minor longways; moderate.

dance & tune: Thompson. Lord Howe had one other dance named after him, Lord Howe's Hornpipe, by Fishar, published by Rutherford in 1778; this dance proved so popular in America that the name had to be changed so as not to honor an enemy, even a friendly enemy, so it is now known as Fisher's (sic) Hornpipe; James A. Fishar was ballet-master at Covent Garden Opera House, London.

1-8	Mirror hey.
9-16	Take six hands and slip left for 8 counts and slip back to the right.
17-24	Partners set and change places; repeat back to places.
25-32	1s cross over and cast below the 2s (2s moving up) and cross back to proper sides with two hands. 1s and 2s do rights and lefts quickly, two counts per change, four changes.

LORD MAYOR'S DELIGHT

16-bar duple-minor longways; easy.

dance: Arnold MS, ca.1790; tune: Playford 14th edition. Miss Arnold was one of Griffiths' dance students in Rhode island, so she probably received this dance from him, and in fact it may have been included in his now-lost first book, published in New Haven in 1786.

1-8	1s cast off (2s move up); partners set; circle once around to the left.
9-16	Partners set, change places by right hands, set and change back by left hands.

LORD MACDONALD'S REEL
32-bar triple-minor longways; moderate-difficult.
dance: William Campbell's 8th book, ca.1790; tune: Skipwith MS, 1790s.

1-8	1s set and cast off (others move up), set and cast back up (others move down).
9-16	1s go down the middle, come back and cast off (2s moving up).
17-24	1s set to first corners and turn them once around with 2 hands in 4 counts, then set to and turn second corners.
25-32	1 man hey with the 3s while 1 woman hey with the 2s; 1s end in second place proper.

LOVE & A BOTTLE
32-bar triple-minor longways; moderate-difficult.
dance & tune: Playford vol.II.

x2

x2

1-8	1 man dances a figure-8 through the 2 & 3 men WHILE 1 woman dances a figure-8 down through the 2s (she crosses in front of her partner to do this).
9-16	1s cast, then 1 man turns 3 man once around with 2 hands while 1 & 3 women do likewise; partners set and turn single.
17-24	1s turn first corners around by right hand, then second corners by the left, ending improper.
25-32	1s set and change places; partners pattacake and turn single.

LOVE & OPPORTUNITY

32-bar triple-minor longways; moderate.
dance & tune: Thompson IV; mentioned in Champlin MS, 1781.

1-8	1s and 2s dance a right-hand star and a left-hand star back.
9-16	1s go down the middle, come back and cast off (2s moving up).
17-24	1s turn first corners once around with 2 hands, then turn second corners once around with 2 hands.
25-32	1s lead out at the sides (lead out between 2 & 3 women, separate and cast in around the ends ; lead out between 2 & 3 men, separate and cast in around ends to progressed places proper).

LOVE'S TRIUMPH

48-bar triple or difficult duple-minor longways; moderate-difficult.
dance & tune: Playford vol.II; the dance is named after an opera with music by Cesarini that opened in London in 1708, but whether this lovely tune was written by him or not is unknown.

1-8	1s & 2s set & turn single; circle to the left half way around and fall back.
9-16	1s & 3s set & turn single; circle to the left half way around and fall back.
17-24	1s cast up into second places (3s move down); partners dos à dos and turn single.
25-32	1s and 2s dance rights & lefts, four changes, starting with partners facing.
33-40	1 man turn 3 woman by the right while 1 woman turn 2 man by the right; then 1 man turn 3 man by the left while 1 woman turn 2 woman by the left; 1s end improper in second places.
41-48	1s lead up through the 2s and cast, then crossing over down through the 3s cast back up to middle places while 2s and 3s turn half way around on the last 4 counts to get proper.

THE LOVER IN DISTRESS
24-bar triple-minor longways; moderate.
dance: Griffiths I, 1788; tune: Defeat of Burgoyne, Brown U. MS; since the original tune has not been found, the substitute has been chosen because Burgoyne considered himself quite a lover, and because that tune's dance has been lost, apparently one of the most popular dances of the Americans during the War of Independence; until recent years, the dance survived on a pack of cards that is now lost.

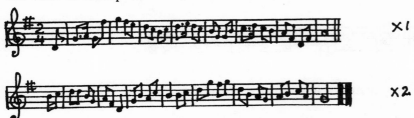

1-8	Mirror hey, 1s on the improper sides, to end in progressed places proper .
9-16	Take hands along the lines and set twice; partners turn once around with 2 hands.
17-24	All face up and chasser 4 steps to the left, rigadoon, chasser back and rigadoon.

THE MACARONI
32-bar duple-minor longways; moderate.
dance: Griffiths II, 1794; tune: Turner MS, etc.; the Macaronis were wealthy young Englishmen who had made a tour of Italy and returned putting on airs and wearing foppish clothing and hairstyles.

1-8	Partners set twice and turn once around with 2 hands.
9-16	1s go down the middle, come back and cast off (2s moving up).
17-24	Circle to the left for 4 counts and back to the right; take hands along the lines and set twice.
25-32	1s and 2s dance rights & lefts, four changes, starting with partners facing.

MARGERY CREE [sic MAGE ON A CREE]

32-bar duple-minor longways; moderate.
dance: A New Academy, 1795; tune: Playford 1st edition, 1651; the dance is unrelated to the Playford dance of almostg a centry and a half earlier.

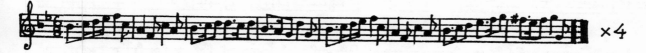

1-8	Partners side to right shoulders, then turn once around with right hands.
9-16	[Partners side to left shoulders and turn once around with left hands].
17-24	Partners turn half way around with 2 hands, set, complete the turn and set again.
25-32	Three changes of rights & lefts; turn single cloverleaf.

MARIONETTES COTILLION LONGWAYS

24-bar duple-minor longways; moderate.
dance: Shepley MS, 1794; tune: Trinity College, Hartford MS.

1-8	1s and 2s circle to the left and circle back to the right.
9-16	1s go down the middle, come back and cast off (2s moving up).
17-24	1s and 2s dance rights & lefts, four changes, starting with partners facing.

THE MARLBOROUGH
44-bar duple-minor longways with part in triple time calling for minuet step; moderate.
dance & tune: Neal, 1726; tune in Parkman MS, 1720.

1-6	1s cross & cast and dance half a figure-8 up through the 2s.
7-12	2s cross & cast and dance half a figure-8 up through the 1s.
13-20	First corners balancer twice and turn once around with 2 hands.
21-28	Second corners do likewise.
29-32	1s & 2s circle 6 walking steps to the left and back to the right.
33-44	1s face up, take near hands and lead through a whole figure-8 around the 2s, starting first around the 2 man; the original directions called for the minuet step, although that is not necessary.

MARY GRAY
24-bar duple-minor longways; moderate.
dance & tune: Frobischer MS, 1793.

X1

X2

1-8	1s and 2s dance a right-hand star and a left-hand star back.
9-16	1s go down the middle, come back and cast off (2s moving up).
17-24	1s and 2s dance rights & lefts, four changes, starting with partners facing.

MERICK'S GRACES
32-bar duple-minor longways, possibly a strathspey; moderate.
dance: Champlin MS, 1781; tune: The Graces, Thompson, 1780.

1-8   1 & 2 men take near hands, lead through the women, separate and cast back to places;
1 & 2 women do likewise.

9-16   1s cross & cast, remaining improper (2s move up); 2s dance half a figure-8 down through the 1s.

17-24   First corners set; second corners set; partners turn half way around by right hands and turn single.

25-32   1s and 2s dance rights & lefts, four changes, starting with partners facing.

MERRILY DANCED THE QUAKER
40-bar triple-minor longways; moderate-difficult.
dance: Bowman (Scots) MS, ca.1760; tune: Gillespie (Scots) MS, 1768; tune in various American MSS ca.1800; Quakers were, of course, not supposed to dance.

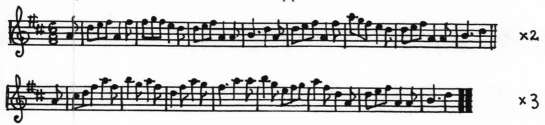

1-8   1s take near hands and set twice to the 2 woman, then set twice to the 2 man.

9-16   1s lead down the middle and come back crossing over and cast improper (2s move up).

17-24   1s cross and cast again below the 3s, turn once around with 2 hands and lead up to face first corners.

25-32   1s set to first corners and turn them once around with 2 hands in 4 counts, then set to and turn second corners.

33-40   1s dance right-shoulder heys for 3 on the improper sides, ending in progressed places proper.

MERRY & WISE
32-bar triple or duple-minor longways; moderate.
dance & tune: Johnson VI, 1751; mentioned in Champlin MS, 1781.

1-8	1s cast off in 8 counts (2s move up on 5–8); 1s turn once around with 2 hands.
9-16	1s circle with the couple below around to the left 8 counts and back to the right.
17-24	1s dance a whole figure-8 up through the 2s.
25-32	1s and 2s dance rights & lefts, four changes, starting with partners facing.

THE MERRY DANCERS
32-bar duple-minor longways; moderate.
dance & tune: Johnson III, 1744; tune found in Aborn and Carroll MSS.

1-8	1s lead down through the 2s (2s cast up), cross over and turn single. 2s lead down through the 1s (1s cast up), cross over and turn single.
9-16	1s cross back and dance a whole figure-8 down through the 2s.
17-24	2s cross back and dance a whole figure-8 up through the 1s.
25-32	Partners pattacake and turn single cloverleaf; neighbors pattacake; 1s cast off (2s move up).

THE MILITARY ASSEMBLY
32-bar triple or duple-minor longways; moderate.
dance: Shepley MS, 1794 and Arnold MS, ca.1790; tune: Military Association, Longman, 1781. The dance was mentioned in Nancy Shippen's diary, ca.1783, and its directions were on a now-lost pack of cards of about the same date.

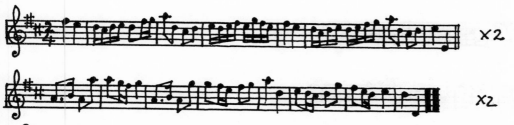

1-8	1s turn once and a half around by the right, and cast off in 8 counts (2s move up on 5–8).
9-16	1s turn once and a half around by the left, and cast off in 8 counts (next couple move up on 5–8).
17-24	1s lead up to the top, set and cast off (3s move down).
25-32	1s and 2s dance rights & lefts, four changes, starting with partners facing.

THE MILITIA
32-bar triple-minor longways; moderate.
dance & tune: Thompson II, 1764. The word Militia was common in early America and very uncommon in England, which suggests that the dance may have had an American origin.

1-8	1s turn once around by the right and cast off (2s move up).
9-16	1s turn once around by the left and cast oppositely (1 man cast down and stand between the 3s while 1 woman cast back up to stand between the 2s).
17-24	Set twice in lines of three across the set; 1s cast back to middle places.
25-32	1s and 2s dance rights & lefts, four changes, starting with partners facing.

MISS ARNOLD'S DELIGHT

32-bar duple-minor longways; easy.

dance: Griffiths I, 1788; tune: Miss Ash's Delight, Johnson IV; Miss Arnold was presumably Griffiths' student who probably wrote the Arnold dance MS in the Rhode Island Historical Society.

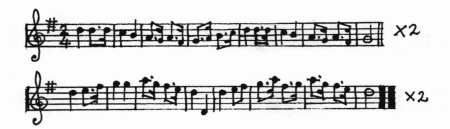

1-8	1s go down the outside for 8 counts, turn and come back.
9-16	1s and 2s circle to the left and circle back to the right.
17-24	1s go down the middle, come back and cast off (2s moving up).
25-32	Partners turn by the right, then turn by the left.

MISS MACDONALD'S REEL

32-bar duple-minor longways; moderate.

dance & tune: Thompson, 1793; mentioned in Champlin MS, 1781, a dozen years before it was published.

1-8	1s turn by the right and cast off into 2nd place (2s move up).
9-16	1s turn once around by the left and cast back up (2s move down).
17-24	1s go down the middle, come back and cast off (2s moving up).
25-32	1s and 2s dance rights & lefts, four changes, starting with partners facing.

MISS SALLY'S ALLEMANDE
32-bar triple-minor longways; moderate.
dance: Miss Sally's Fancy, Walsh Caledonian, 1754; tune: Skipwith MS, 1790s.

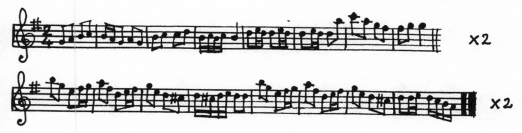

1-8	1s go down the middle, come back and cast off (2s moving up).
9-16	1s lead down the middle again, come back and cast off (next couple move up).
17-24	Circle once around to the left; 1s lead up to the top (others move down) and cast off to progressed places.
25-32	Partners allemande right and then allemande left.

THE MONCKTON or BRITISH WHITE FEATHERS
40-bar triple or duple-minor longways; moderate.
dance & tune: Cantelo, 1785, written by Colonel Cosmo Gordon. Monckton was the name of two brothers, officers with the British forces in America. Henry was killed at the battle of Monmouth, 1778, and Robert was captured the same year in Long Island and soon exchanged; the dance probably refers to the latter, as "white feathers" often hints at cowardice, a possible attribute of someone who was captured.

1-8	Second corners set twice and turn once around by the right.
9-16	First corners do likewise.
17-24	1s go down the middle, come back and cast off (2s moving up).
25-32	1s and the couple below circle to the left and circle back to the right.
33-40	1s and 2s dance rights & lefts, four changes, starting with partners facing.

THE MONMOUTH or THE VICTORY

32-bar duple-minor longways; easy.

dance & tune: Cantelo, 1785. The title refers to the battle of Monmouth, NJ at the end of June, 1778. How it can be described as a victory, however, is anyone's guess, for although British General Clinton managed to bring most of his army safely to New York (his objective after evacuating Philadelphia), he lost about 2000 men to battle and desertion while the Americans lost fewer than 400.

1-8	1s and 2s dance a right-hand star and a left-hand star back.
9-16	1s go down the middle, come back and cast off (2s moving up).
17-24	1s and 2s dance rights & lefts, four changes, starting with partners facing.
25-32	All set twice; partners turn once around with 2 hands.

MONYMUSK

32-bar triple-minor longways strathspey; moderate.

dance & tune: Frobischer MS, 1793. The dance, written about 1775, was originally named Sir Archibald Grant of Monemusk (sic) Strathspey Reel, quite a mouthful.

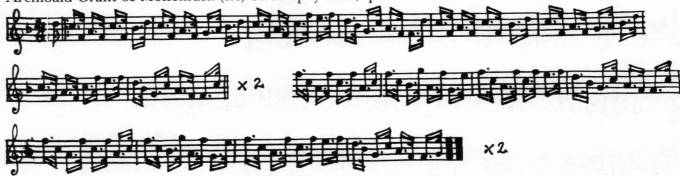

1-4	1s turn by the right and cast off into 2nd place (2s move up).
5-8	1s turn by the left once and a quarter around and fall into places thus: the woman between the 2s and the man between the 3s.
9-16	Set once in lines across; 1s turn by the right three-quarters around to end in middle places improper; set once in lines on the sides; 1s turn by the right half way around to end proper.
17-24	All 3 couples circle to the left and circle back to the right.
25-32	1s lead out at the sides (lead out between 2 & 3 women, separate and cast in around the ends ; lead out between 2 & 3 men, separate and cast in around ends to progressed places proper).

MORGAN RATTLER

32-bar duple-minor longways; easy.

dance: Moore/Ridgely MS, 1790s; tune: Carroll MS; the title probably refers to Virginia's General Daniel Morgan, whose sharpshooting riflemen were as dangerous as a rattlesnake to the British in the War of Independence.

1-8	Partners set and change sides, set and change back.
9-16	First corners allemande right; second corners allemande left.
17-24	1s go down the middle, come back and cast off (2s moving up).
24-32	1s and 2s circle to the left and circle back to the right.

THE MORNING GAZETTE

24 or 32-bar duple-minor longways; easy.

dance: Griffiths I, 1788; tune: The Morning Dance, published by Thompson in 1787, is the same dance, so its tune is used here; the Thompson dance adds the last figure, omitted by accident in the Griffiths.

1-8	1s set twice to the 2 woman, then all 3 circle once around to the left.
9-16	1s set twice to the 2 man, then all 3 circle once around to the left.
17-24	1s go down the middle, come back and cast off (2s moving up).
25-32	Partners allemande right and then allemande left.

MORRIS' DANCE
32-bar duple-minor longways; moderate-easy.
dance: Griffiths I, 1788; tune: Playford (probably not the right tune, but . . .).

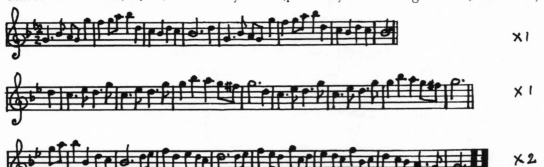

x1

x1

x2

1-8	Second corners turn once around with 2 hands; first corners do likewise.
9-16	1s go down the middle, come back and cast off (2s moving up).
17-24	Partners take right hands to change places and set, then left hands to change back and set.
25-32	1s and 2s circle to the left and circle back to the right.

MOUNT VERNON
32-bar triple-minor longways; moderate.
dance: An Elegant Collection . . . by W.D., 1798; tune: Mansfield, CT MS. Mount Vernon, named after his brother's hero, British Admiral Edward Vernon, was George Washington's lovely mansion near Alexandria, VA. It has a handsome ballroom, and is open to the public.

1- 8	1s & 2s join hands in a tight ring and chasser 4 steps down the middle and rigadoon; partners turn once and a half around with 2 hands.
9-16	Repeat back to places.
17-24	1s chasser down the middle and cast out around the 3s into second place (2s move up); all six circle left half way around.
25-32	Take hands along the lines, set and rigadoon; all six complete the circle to the left.

MRS. S. DOUGLAS' REEL
32-bar triple-minor longways; moderate.
dance & tune: Cantelo, 1785, written by Colonel Cosmo Gordon.

1-8	Partners set and change sides, set and change back again.
9-16	1s chasser down the middle six steps and back up for 2 steps into second places (2s having moved up); partners turn once around with two hands.
17-24	First corners set and turn once around with 2 hands quickly (turn in 4 counts); then second corners do likewise.
25-32	1s lead out at the sides (lead out between 2 & 3 women, separate and cast in around the ends; lead out between 2 & 3 men, separate and cast in around ends to progressed places proper).

MRS. LT.-COL. JOHNSON'S REEL
32-bar triple-minor longways; moderate.
dance & tune: Cantelo, 1785, written by Colonel Cosmo Gordon.

1-8	1s and 2s dance a right-hand star and a left-hand star back.
9-16	1s go down the middle, come back and cast off (2s moving up).
17-24	First corners set and turn once around with 2 hands quickly (turn in 4 counts); then second corners do likewise.
25-32	Partners set and change places taking right hands, set and change back taking left hands.

THE MUNICHAUSEN

32-bar triple or duple-minor longways; moderate-difficult.

dance & tune: Cantelo, 1785; the title probably refers to one of the German mercenaries fighting for the British.

1-8	1s go down the middle, come back and cast off (2s moving up).
9-16	1s go down the outside for 8 counts, turn and come back.
17-24	1s set to partner, set to first corners, set to partner, and set to second corners.
25-32	1s circle to the left once around with the couple below, then quick rights & lefts with the couple above, 2 counts per side.

THE NEGROE

28-bar triple or duple-minor longways; moderate-difficult.

dance & tune: Johnson VI, 1751. Since Africans were a great rarity in Britain and very numerous in parts of America, it is likely that this dance originated in America.

1-8	first corners set and turn once around with 2 hands in 4 counts, then second corners set and turn.
9-16	1s cross over 2 couples (cross by the right, cast, cross over again by the right and cast again to below the 2nd standing couple); 1s lead up to the top.
17-22	1s set, cast off (2s move up), quickly lead down through the couple below and cast off to progressed places.
23-28	1s & 2s dance rights & lefts, 3 counts per side.

NEW CITY MILITIA
32-bar triple or duple-minor longways; moderate.
dance & tune: Dodd, 1795. The New City in question was Washington, DC.

1-8   1s promenade down the outside on the men's side, dance in below the second standing couple and turn once around with 2 hands.

9-16   1s promenade up the outside on the women's side, come into original places and turn once around with 2 hands.

17-24   1s lead down the middle through two standing couples and cast up one place (2s move up).

25-32   1s and 2s dance rights & lefts, four changes, starting with partners facing.

NEW CONSTITUTION
32-bar duple-minor longways; moderate.
dance: Shepley MS, 1794; tune: American MS, ca.1800.

1-8   1s go down the outside for 8 counts, turn and come back.

9-16   Partners set; 1s allemande right for 4 counts; partners set; 1s allemande left back.

17-24   1s go down the middle, come back and cast off (2s moving up).

25-32   1s and 2s dance rights & lefts, four changes, starting with partners facing.

NEW ENGLAND

24-bar duple-minor longways; moderate.
dance & tune: Playford.

1-8	1s cast off and turn single oppositely, cast back up and turn single.
9-16	1s dance a full figure-8 down through the 2s.
17-24	1s cross & cast (2s move up) and turn one and a half times around with 2 hands to proper sides.

NEW ENGLAND LADY/LA NOUVELLE ANGLOISE

32-bar duple-minor longways; moderate.
dance & tune: 12 Contredansen voor de Viool en Dwars Fluyt . . ., Amsterdam, 1771; tune in Turner MS, 1788.

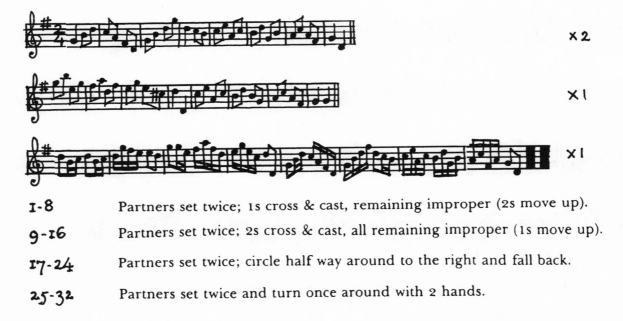

1-8	Partners set twice; 1s cross & cast, remaining improper (2s move up).
9-16	Partners set twice; 2s cross & cast, all remaining improper (1s move up).
17-24	Partners set twice; circle half way around to the right and fall back.
25-32	Partners set twice and turn once around with 2 hands.

NEW JERSEY

32-bar duple-minor longways; moderate.
dance: Moore/Ridgely MS, 1790s; tune: Carroll MS.

1-8	First corners set twice and turn once around with 2 hands.
9-16	Second corners set twice and turn once around with 2 hands.
17-24	1s go down the middle, come back and cast off (2s moving up).
25-32	1s and 2s dance rights & lefts, four changes, starting with partners facing.

NEW LONDON ASSEMBLY

40 or 32-bar triple or duple-minor longways; moderate.
dance: Shepley MS, 1794; tune: Turner MS, 1788. This is likely to have been included in Griffiths' now-lost first book published at New Haven, 1786.

1-8	Partners set; circle 4 slips around to the left; set; circle 4 slips back to the right. Note: this same figure in the original instructions was repeated after the cast off, so it has been omitted the second time here to avoid being tedious.
9-16	1s go down the middle, come back and cast off (2s moving up).
17-24	Partners turn by the right, then turn by the left.
25-32	1s and 2s dance rights & lefts, four changes, starting with partners facing.

THE NEW-RIGGED SHIP

32-bar triple or duple-minor longways; moderate.
dance: Wilson, 1816; tune: Murphey MS, 1790.

Ships in the eighteenth century had to have their rigs replaced (the rope and some of the spars) practically every time they expected to undertake a long voyage.

1-8	1 Woman leads the other two women counterclockwise around the three men and back to places.
9-16	1 Man leads the other two men clockwise around the three women.
17-24	The 1s and 3s poussette clockwise around the 2s.
25-36	The 1s lead down the middle through the 3s and cast up to second place, the 2s moving up. Partners do a two-hand turn.

THE NEW RUSSIA DANCE

32-bar duple-minor longways; moderate.
dance: Griffiths I, 1788; tune: Thompson, 1782.

1-8	Second corners set & turn single; first corners set & turn single.
9-16	Partners take near hands and neighbors face; set twice; circle once around to the left.
17-24	1s dance down the middle, turn as a couple (man backing up), come back, cast off improper (2s move up) and cross back to proper sides.
25-32	1s and 2s dance rights & lefts, four changes, starting with partners facing.

THE NEW STAR
24-bar duple-minor longways; moderate-easy.
dance: Griffiths I, 1788; tune, Johnson V.

1-8 1s turn once around by the right and cast off below two standing couples (2s do not move).

9-16 1s set, dance up the middle to the top, set and cast off (2s move up).

17-24 1s and 2s circle to the left and circle back to the right.

NEW YORK or THE KING'S MAGGOT
32-bar triple-minor longways;   moderate to difficult.
dance & tune: Playford about 1718.

1-8 1s cross and cast below the 2s (the 2s moving up) and take two hands to cross back to proper sides. 1s then lead down through the 3s an cast up to middle place; 1s do a two-hand turn.

9-16 1s turn contrary corners (first corner by right hand, partner left, second corner right, partner left).

17-24 1 Man does figure-8 around the 3s while 1 Woman does figure-8 around the 2s. Then they pass by right shoulders and the 1 Man does a hey with the 2s while the 1 Woman heys with the 3s.

25-32 Partners back-to-back. 1s and 2s dance rights & lefts, four changes, starting with partners facing.

NEWPORT ASSEMBLY

32 or 40-bar duple-minor longways; moderate.
dance & tune: Thompson, 1780; possibly written by African-born Newport Gardner, who had had previous dance compositions published in England.

1-8	Take hands with neighbor and set twice; partners change in 8 counts, taking right hands.
9-16	Take hands with neighbor and set twice; partners change in 8 counts, taking right hands.
17-24	1s and 2s dance a right-hand star and a left-hand star back.
25-32	1s cross & cast (2s move up) and dance half a figure-8 up through the 2s.
33-40	Partners allemande right and then allemande left.

NEWS FROM AMERICA

16-bar duple-minor longways; moderate.
dance & tune: Fishar.

1-8	Dance two changes of rights & lefts and circle to the left back to places.
9-16	First corners change; second corners change; 1s cast up; partners change and 1s cast down all in 4 counts.

NIGHTINGALE'S FANCY

32-bar duple-minor longways; moderate-easy.
dance: Griffiths I, 1788; tune: A New Contredance, by Henri Capron, published in Moller & Capron's Monthly Numbers #3, Philadelphia, 1793. The Nightingale family were prominent Providence merchants.

is improper

1-8	1s go down the outside for 8 counts, turn and come back.
9-16	1s go down the middle, come back and cast off (2s moving up).
17-24	1s and 2s circle to the left and circle back to the right.
25-32	Neighbors take hands chasser out 4 steps, rigadoon, chasser back and rigadoon.

NOSEGAY

32-bar triple or duple-minor longways; moderate.
dance: Griffiths I, 1788; tune: Carroll MS; tune also known as The Nook of Fife.

1-8	Neighbors take hands (but not partners) and dance a circle half way around to fall back on the opposite sides, then reverse direction back to places.
9-16	1s go down the middle, come back and cast off (2s moving up).
17-24	1s and the couple below dance a right-hand star and a left-hand star back.
25-32	1s and 2s dance rights & lefts, four changes, starting with partners facing.

NOVA SCOTIA
32-bar duple-minor longways; moderate.
dance & tune: Thompson I, 1758.

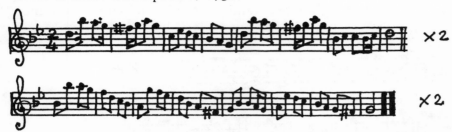

1-8	Partners set twice and change sides.
9-16	Partners set twice and change back again.
17-24	1s go down the middle, come back and cast off (2s moving up).
25-32	1s and 2s dance rights & lefts, four changes, starting with partners facing.

OSCAR & MALVINA
24-bar triple or duple-minor longways; moderate.
dance & tune: Frobischer MS, 1793.

1-8	Partners set and change sides, set and change back again.
9-16	1s dance down the middle for 8 counts (2s move up), come back up to progressed places in 4 counts and overhead-allemande in 4 counts.
17-24	1s turn first corners once around with 2 hands, then turn second corners once around with 2 hands.

OYSTER RIVER

24-bar duple-minor longways; moderate.
dance: Muzzey MS, 1795; tune: The Oysterwife's Rant, Murphey MS, 1790.

1-8	First corners change; second corners change; right-hand star half way around back to places.
9-16	1s go down the middle, come back and cast off (2s moving up).
17-24	1s and 2s dance rights & lefts, four changes, starting with partners facing.

THE PANTHEON

32-bar triple-minor longways; moderate.
dance & tune: Thompson, 1773; tune appears in Skipwith MS, 1790s. The title refers to the splendid domed church of Sainte-Geneviève built in Paris by Soufflot in the 1760s, which was nicknamed the Panthéon.

1-8	1s circle once around with 2 woman, then 1s circle with 2 man.
9-16	1s cross over, dance down the outside improper and come in below the 3s crossing back; dance up to the top and cast off (2s move up).
17-24	1 woman circle once around with the 2s while the 1 man circle once around with the 3s; then the three men circle while the three women circle once around.
25-32	1s lead out at the sides (lead out between 2 & 3 women, separate and cast in around the ends ; lead out between 2 & 3 men, separate and cast in around ends to progressed places proper).

LA PARISIENNE
32-bar duple-minor longways; moderate.
dance & tune: Trois Rivieres MS, ca.1765; tune completed by Ticknor & Millar.

1-8	Partners set, rigadoon and turn once around with 2 hands.
9-16	All dance forward a double (using contretemps step) and back; men face down while women face up; chasser 4 steps across and rigadoon.
17-24	All chasser back and rigadoon; 1s lead down the middle to progressed places while 2s cast up; all balancer.
25-32	Partners allemande right and then allemande left.

PHILADELPHIA REEL
32-bar triple-minor or three-couple set; moderate.
dance: Weeks MS, 1783; tune: Jack's Alive (as specified in the MS).

1-8	1s dance down the outside (2s move up) and come back only to progressed places.
9-16	1s and 2s dance a right-hand star and a left-hand star back.
17-24	1s set to first corners, set to partners (may be best to be improper at this stage), set to second corners and set to partner.
25-32	1s lead out at the sides (lead out between 2 & 3 women, separate and cast in around the ends ; lead out between 2 & 3 men, separate and cast in around ends to progressed places proper).

THE PLEASURE OF LOVE
32-bar duple-minor longways; moderate-easy.
dance: Griffiths I, 1788; tune: in Ralph's operetta The Fashionable Lady. The tune is also known as Through the Wood, Laddy. James Ralph was one of America's first music composers; he was born in Philadelphia, but did most of his work for the London stage.

1-8	1s and 2s dance a right-hand star and a left-hand star back.
9-16	1s go down the outside for 8 counts, turn and come back.
17-24	1s go down the middle, come back and cast off (2s moving up).
25-32	1s and 2s circle to the left and circle back to the right.

THE PLEASURE OF PROVIDENCE
32-bar triple-minor longways; moderate.
dance: Griffiths I, 1788; tune: The Pleasures of the Town, Thompson.

1-8	1s dance down the outside and come in below the second standing couple; chasser up the middle to places; partners set.
9-16	1s and 2s dance a right-hand star and a left-hand star back.
17-24	1s go down the middle, come back and cast off (2s moving up).
25-32	1s and 2s dance rights & lefts, four changes, starting with partners facing.

133

THE POOR SOLDIER

24-bar triple or duple-minor longways; moderate.
dance: Griffiths I, 1788; tune: Adams MS; George Washington stated that his favorite operetta was Shield's The Poor Soldier, 1783, after whom the dance was named.

1-8	Second corners set & turn single; first corners do likewise.
9-16	1s go down the middle, come back and cast off (2s moving up).
17-24	1 man take 2 hands with the man below and chasser out 4 steps and back; then the women do likewise.

PORT ROYAL

32-bar duple-minor longways; moderate.
dance & tune: Neal, 1726. Port Royal was the principal seaport of Jamaica until it was destroyed by a terrible earthquake late in the seventeenth century, which many people thought was the tangible wrath of God upon the incredibly licentious lifestyle there.

1-8	1s dance half a figure-8 down through the 2s, set and cast off improper (2s move up).
9-16	2s dance half a figure-8 down through the 1s, set and cast off improper (1s move up).
17-24	Partners pattacake and turn single (cloverleaf), then right-hand star half way around and fall back.
25-32	Neighbors turn once around by the right; partners turn once around by the left.

THE PRESIDENT

40-bar duple-minor longways; moderate.
dance: Muzzey MS, 1795; tune: The President's March, Beck MS.

1-8	Second corners set & turn single; first corners set & turn single.
9-16	1s go down the outside for 8 counts, turn and come back.
17-24	1s go down the middle, come back and cast off (2s moving up).
25-32	1s and 2s dance a right-hand star and a left-hand star back.
33-40	1s and 2s dance rights & lefts, four changes, starting with partners facing.

PRINCE EDWARD'S FANCY

40-bar triple-minor longways; moderate.
dance & tune: Frobischer MS, 1793; Prince Edward, who was stationed in Canada for several years, was created Duke of Kent in 1799 and became the father of Queen Victoria. He was an avid dancer.

1-8	1 woman set twice to 2 man and turn 3 man once around with 2 hands.
9-16	1 man set twice to 2 woman and turn 3 woman once around with 2 hands.
17-24	1s go down the middle, come back and cast off (2s moving up).
25-32	Partners allemande right and then allemande left.
33-40	1s turn first corners once around with 2 hands, then turn second corners once around with 2 hands.

THE QUEEN'S DELIGHT
20-bar triple or duple-minor longways; moderate.
dance & tune: Playford 13th edition, 1706; tune in Parkman MS, 1720.

1-8	1s clap once (or pattacake if there is time) and cast off (2s do not move up); 1s lead down through the couple below and cast back up to progressed places.
9-14	1s and 2s dance rights & lefts, four changes, starting with partners facing.
15-20	1s lead up through the top (4 counts) and cast off in 8 counts (2s move up on last 4 counts).

QUESNAY
40-bar triple-minor longways; moderate.
dance: Griffiths I, 1788; tune: Playford vol.II, 4th edition. Alexandre-Marie Quesnay Chevalier de Beaurepaire was Griffiths' employer for many years.

1-8	1s lead down the middle (4 counts), set below the 3s and cast (8 counts) back to places.
9-16	3s lead up the middle, set above the 1s and cast back to places.
17-24	1s cross & cast, cross and cast again.
25-32	1s cross (4 counts) and cast up (8 counts) to second places and turn half way around by the right to proper sides.
33-40	1s and 2s dance rights & lefts, four changes, starting with partners facing.

THE RAKES OF RODNEY
32-bar triple-minor longways; moderate.
dance: Shepley MS, 1794; tune: Rodney for Ever, Carroll MS. Rodney's crushing victory over the French in 1782 helped enable the British to claim that while they lost the American colonies, they beat the French, Dutch, Spanish and the rebels in India all at the same time.

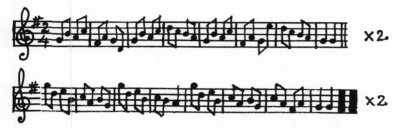

1-8	1s go down the outside for 8 counts, turn and come back.
9-16	1s hey on the opposite sides.
17-24	1s go down the middle, come back and cast off (2s moving up).
25-32	1s and 2s dance rights & lefts, four changes, starting with partners facing.

RANGER'S WEDDING
24-bar triple-minor longways; moderate.
dance & tune: Johnson VI, 1751. Rangers were soldiers skilled in wilderness lore in America, especially those led by Sir William Johnson of Johnstown, NY, so the dance may be of American origin.

1-8	1 man, followed by 1 woman, cast off (2s move up), dance in below the 2 man and dance clockwise around the 3 man to end in second places improper.
9-16	1 woman, followed by 1 man, dance down the middle, out below the 3 woman, counterclockwise around her and up the middle to first places proper (2s move down).
17-24	1s face down and 2s face up; turn once around with 2 hands; 1s cross & cast (2s move up) and turn half way around with 2 hands to proper sides.

THE RETREAT OF CLINTON
32-bar triple-minor longways; moderate-difficult.
dance & tune: The Retreat, Thompson II; The Retreat of Clinton was a dance popular during the War of Independence and its directions were preserved until recently on a pack of playing cards (now lost). It is doubtful whether it was really the Thompson dance renamed, but that is the nearest that can presently be reached.

 x 2

 x 2

1-8	1s set, cast and set twice.
9-16	1 man cast down while 1 woman cast up to form lines of three across the set; take hands and set; 1s turn three-quarters around with 2 hands to end in second places improper.
17-24	Take hands and set twice in lines on the sides; then 1s set to first corners and then to second corners.
25-32	1s circle once around to the left with the 3s, then dance quick rights & lefts with the 2s (2 counts per side).

RHODE ISLAND MARCH DANCE
32-bar duple-minor longways; moderate.
dance: Griffiths II, 1794; tune: Col. Shepley MS.

1-8	1s and 2s dance a right-hand star and a left-hand star back.
9-16	1s go down the middle, come back and cast off (2s moving up).
17-24	Taking hands along the lines, set twice; partners turn once around with 2 hands.
25-32	1s and 2s dance rights & lefts, four changes, starting with partners facing.

RICKETT'S HORNPIPE

32-bar duple-minor longways; easy.
dance: Moore-Ridgely MS, 1790s; tune: Carroll MS.

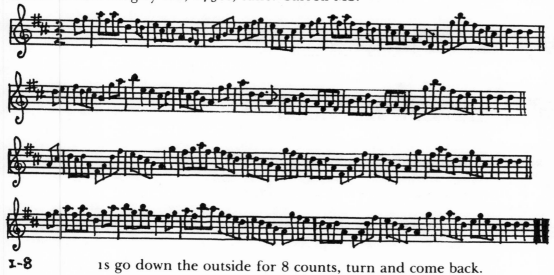

1-8	1s go down the outside for 8 counts, turn and come back.
9-16	1s and 2s dance a right-hand star and a left-hand star back.
17-24	1s go down the middle, come back and cast off (2s moving up).
25-32	1s and 2s circle to the left and circle back to the right.

THE ROSE

32-bar duple-minor longways; moderate.
dance: Muzzey MS 1795; tune: Beck MS. The title may refer to the 24-gun British frigate of that name, whose anti-smuggling activities in Rhode Island in 1775 caused such hardship there that Rhode Island persuaded the Continental Congress to found the American Navy. The author built a full-sized, operational copy of the ship in 1969–70, now based in Bridgeport, CT.

1-8	Second corners set twice; then 1 man take near hands with partner and lead counter-clockwise around the 2 woman and back to places.
9-16	First corners set twice; then 1 woman take near hands with partner and lead clockwise around 2 man and back to places.
17-24	1s go down the middle, come back and cast off (2s moving up).
25-32	1s and 2s dance rights & lefts, four changes, starting with partners facing.

ROSINA

16 or 24-bar duple-minor longways; moderate.
dance & tune: Frobischer MS, 1793. The title refers to a popular operetta written by Shield in 1783.

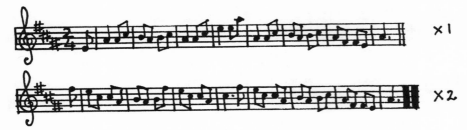

1-8	1s and 2s dance a right-hand star and a left-hand star back.
9-16	1s go down the middle, come back and cast off (2s moving up).
17-24	1s and 2s dance rights & lefts, four changes, starting with partners facing.

THE ROYAL QUICKSTEP

24-bar triple-minor longways; moderate.
dance & tune: Frobishcer MS, 1793.

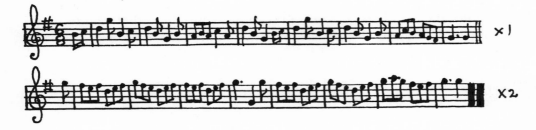

1-8	1s lead down through the 3s (2s following the 1s) and cast back up to places.
9-16	1s cross & cast (2s move up) and turn one and a half times around with 2 hands to proper sides.
17-24	1s and 2s dance rights & lefts, four changes, starting with partners facing.

THE SAINT GEORGE
24-bar duple-minor longways; moderate.
dance & tune: Cantelo, 1785.

1-8   Right-hand star for 4 counts, set, left-hand star back and set.

9-16   1s chasser down the middle for 6 steps and back up for 2 in to progressed places (2s having moved up); take hands along the lines and set twice.

17-24   Circle to the left for 4 counts, set, circle back to the right and set.

THE SEA SIDE
40-bar triple-minor longways;   moderate.
dance & tune: Bride, 1768. This is the earliest piece of music attributed to African-born composer Newport Gardner of Newport, RI; he was 22 years old and had been in America only eight years. The tune is also known as Crookéd Shanks and as Bill of Rights.

1-8   Take hands on the sides, set twice, then half rights & lefts.

9-16   Repeat back to places.

17-28   1s cross & cast (2s move up), set twice and turn one and a half times around with 2 hands to proper sides.

29-40   1 man dance a figure-8 around the couple below while the 1 woman dance similarly around the couple above; 1s turn with 2 hands to places.

SIX-HAND REEL

38-bar three-couple longways set; moderate.
dance: Moore/Ridgely MS, 1790s; tune: Federal Cotillion (as specified in MS; adapted by Gail Ticknor to fit dance).

1-12	1s chasser down the outside to below the 3s and rigadoon; right-hand star with the threes and left-hand star back.
13-24	1s chasser up the outside to the top and rigadoon; right-hand star with the 2s and left-hand star back.
25-36	1s cross & cast, cross & cast, cross & cast up, cross & cast up again to top places proper.
37-38	1s chasser down the middle to the foot (the others moving up), and the dance begins again with a new top couple.

THE SPANIARD

32-bar duple-minor longways; moderate.
dance & tune: Thompson; the dance is given in Champlin MS, 1781.

1-8	First corners set & turn single; partners turn once around with 2 hands.
9-16	Second corners set & turn single; partners turn once around with 2 hands.
17-24	1s go down the middle, come back and cast off (2s moving up).
25-32	1s and 2s circle to the left and circle back to the right.

SPEED THE PLOUGH

32-bar triple or duple-minor longways; moderate-easy.
dance: Fisin, Ode to May, 1799; tune: Skipwith MS, 1790s.

1-8	All 3 couples circle to the left and circle back to the right.
9-16	1s go down the middle, come back and cast off (2s moving up).
17-24	Allemande right first corners, allemande left partners.
25-32	allemande right second corners, and allemande left partners.

SPIRIT OF FRANCE

24-bar duple-minor longways; moderate.
dance: Moore/Ridgely MS, 1790s; tune: Cary MS.

1-8	Partners set and change sides, set and change back again.
9-16	1s go down the middle, come back and cast off (2s moving up).
17-24	1s and 2s dance rights & lefts, four changes, starting with partners facing.

STRATFORD JUBILEE

24-bar duple-minor longways; easy.

dance & tune: Thompson, 1773. The word jubilee means a celebration of some multiple of 25 years' anniversary, and it is not clear which Stratford was celebrating such an anniversary—Shakespeare's Stratford, England, or the Lee family's Stratford Hall Plantation in Virginia (believed to have been designed about 1738 by Peter Harrison) with its handsome ballroom.

1-8	1s go down the outside for 8 counts, turn and come back.
9-16	1s cross by right shoulders, cast, cross again and cast again.
17-24	1s lead up to the top in 8 counts and cast off in 8 counts (2s moving up).

STRUAN ROBERTSON'S STRATHSPEY

40-bar triple-minor longways strathspey; moderate-difficult.

dance & tune: Rutherford, ca.1750; tune in Frobischer MS, 1793.

1-8	1s cast down the outside and come in below the 3s; dance up to the top and cast off (2s move up).
9-16	First corners strathspey set; 1s strathspey set; second corners strathspey set; 1s strathspey set.
17-24	1s turn first corners by right hands, turn partner by the left; 1s turn second corners by right hands, turn partner by the left.
25-32	1 man dance a hey for three with the 3s while 1 woman dance with 2s, then change ends.
33-40	1 man dance a hey for three with the 2s while 1 woman dance with 3s., and end in progressed places proper.

TICONDEROGA

24-bar triple-minor longways; moderate.

dance & tune: Thompshon, 1780. Fort Ticonderoga on Lake Champlain, NY, was built by the French as Fort Carillon. During the War of Independence, in one of the early conflicts of the war, it was captured in May 1775 by Benedict Arnold and Ethan Allen; it was recaptured by the British force led by Burgoyne in 1777, the event probably commemorated in the name of the dance.

1 woman and 3 man turn once around with 2 hands and return to place; 1 man turn 3 woman once around with 2 hands and end standing between the 3s facing up, while 1 woman moves in to stand between the 2s facing down.

Take hands and set once in lines across the set; 1s turn three-quarters around by the right in 4 counts; take hands and set once in lines of three on the sides; 1s turn by the right half way around to end proper.

All 3 couples circle to the left and circle back to the right.

THE TOAST

48-bar triple or duple minor; moderate-difficult.

dance & tune: Feuillet/Essex, 1710.

play AABCBC

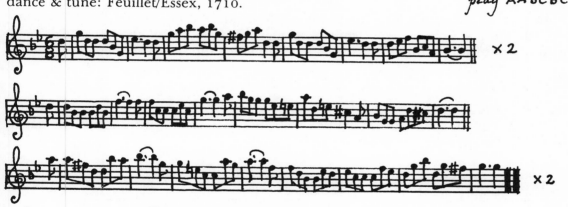

1-8	1s cast off and dance half a figure-8 up through the 2s, then cast off one more place.
9-16	1s cast back up one place and dance half a figure-8 down through the couple below, then cast back up to places.
17-24	All turn single to the left in 8 counts (make big loops), ending in line across facing up, in this order: 1 man, 1 woman, 2 man, 2 woman; take hands in the line and set twice.
25-32	All turn single to the right in 8 counts (make big loops), ending back in original places; circle once around to the left.
33-40	All turn single to the right in 8 counts (make big loops) to end in a standing outward-facing circle; all turn single to the left in 8 counts (make big loops) to return to original places.
41-48	First corners cross; second corners cross; partners turn once and a half around with 2 hands.

TRENCHMORE/THE HUNTING OF THE FOX

Progressive longways set, not necessarily danced to the phrase of the music; best with 6 couples; easy. dance: Playford, 1721. tune: any reel will do; here, The Black Birds Reel, Skipwith MS, 1790s. The dance was already well-known when it was first mentioned in literature, 1564. When it was mentioned early in the seventeenth century by Selden, he said: "then all the company dances [together], lord and groom, lady and kitchen maid, no distinction." In the eighteenth century, it was presumably one of the many dances known as Virginia Reels, and later in the nineteenth century it became known as THE Virginia Reel.

EITHER: partners take near hands and lead up a double and fall back again (twice); OR: take hands along the lines and dance forward a double and fall back again (twice).

Top couple, followed by the others, cast off to the bottom of the set (this was the place that rowdy people reportedly used to dance over tables and chairs!) and lead back up to places.

All partners join near hands and dance a progressive, arched hey, thus: 1s go under the arch made by the 2s, make an arch for the 3s, go under the 4s, etc.; each couple begins the hey when the 1s reach them; couples reaching either end of the set change hands and reverse direction, and the hey continues until all are back in original places.

1 man arm right with partner (first time only, once and a half around), then arm left with 2 woman, right with partner, left with 3 woman, etc., while 1 woman arms left with the respective men, alternating with arming right with partner, until the 1s reach the foot and the dance begins again with new top couple.

TRIO DANCE

32-bar duple-minor longways; moderate-easy.
dance: Griffiths I, 1788; tune: Independence, Cary MS. This is a marriage, in which only the dance survives for one and only the tune for the other.

Take hands along the lines, balancer twice and circle left half way around, falling back on the opposite   sides.

Take hands along the lines, balancer twice and circle right back to places, falling back on the last 4   counts.

1s go down the middle, come back and cast off (2s moving up).

Men face down and women face up; all chasser 4 steps across the set (partners passing face to face);   rigadoon, chasser back and rigadoon.

A TRIP TO ALEXANDRIA

24-bar duple-minor longways; moderate.
dance & tune: Thompson 1799

1-8	1s and 2s dance a right-hand star and a left-hand star back.
9-16	1s go down the middle, come back and cast off (2s moving up).
17-24	1s and 2s circle to the left and circle back to the right.

A TRIP TO ANKERWICK

24-bar duple-minor longways; moderate.
dance & tune: Turner MS, 1788.

1-8	1s go down the outside for 8 counts, turn and come back.
9-16	1s go down the middle, come back and cast off (2s moving up).
17-24	1s and 2s dance rights & lefts, four changes, starting with partners facing.

A TRIP TO BATH

32-bar triple-minor longways; moderate.
dance: Moore/Ridgely MS, 1790s; tune: Thompson I, 1758.

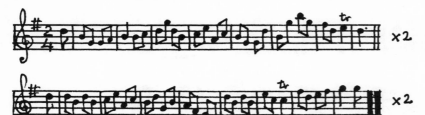

1-8	1s go down the outside for 8 counts, turn and come back.
9-16	1s go down the middle, come back and cast off (2s moving up).
17-24	1s turn first corners once around with 2 hands, then turn second corners once around with 2 hands.
25-32	1s take 2 hands and chasser 4 steps out the men's side, then chasser back 4 steps and turn as many times as necessary to end proper.

A TRIP TO CARLISLE

40-bar duple-minor longways; moderate.
dance & tune: Thompson II; mentioned in Champlin MS, 1781.

1-8	All set twice; half right & lefts.
9-16	All set twice; half right & lefts.
17-24	1s and 2s dance a right-hand star and a left-hand star back.
25-32	1s go down the middle, come back and cast off (2s moving up).
33-40	1s and 2s dance rights & lefts, four changes, starting with partners facing.

A TRIP TO GEORGIA

24-bar triple or duple-minor longways; moderate.
dance & tune: Johnson.

1-8   Take hands along the lines and set; partners pattacake; set again; 2s pattacake, while
1s turn single (man left, woman right).

9-16   1s turn single in the other directions, then cast below 2 standing couples and turn once
around with 2 hands.

17-24   1s lead up to original places, cast off (2s move up) and turn once around with 2 hands.

A TRIP TO GUADELOUPE

40-bar triple or duple-minor longways; moderate.
dance & tune: Thompson II.

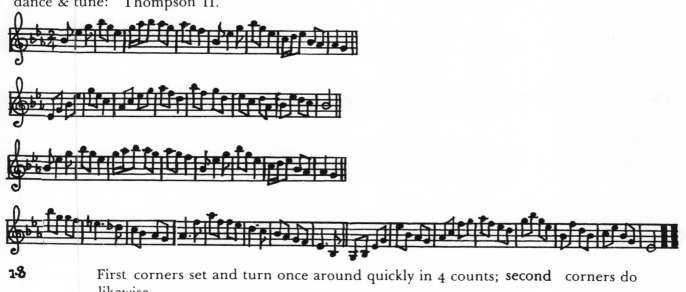

1-8   First corners set and turn once around quickly in 4 counts; **second** corners do
likewise.

9-16   2 man and woman of couple below set and turn (in 4 counts) once around with 2 hands,
then 2 woman and man of couple below do likewise.

17-24   1s cross over 2 couples (cross by the right, cast, cross over again by the right and cast
again to below the 2nd standing couple).

25-32   1s lead up to the top (it is permissible to turn with 2 hands on the way up to fill the
music, or perhaps use the bourree step) and cast off (2s move up).

33-40   1s circle to the left once around with the couple below, then dance quick rights & lefts
with the couple above (2 counts per side).

A TRIP TO HALIFAX

32-bar duple-minor longways; moderate.
dance: Weeks MS, 1783; tune: Cunningham MS.

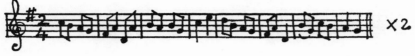

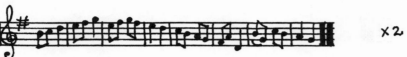

1-8	First corners set twice and turn once around with 2 hands.
9-16	Second corners set twice and turn once around with 2 hands.
17-24	1s cross & cast (2s move up) and turn one and a half times around with 2 hands to proper sides.
25-32	1s and 2s dance rights & lefts, four changes, starting with partners facing.

A TRIP TO KINGSTON

32-bar triple or duple-minor longways; moderate.
dance & tune: Johnson VI, 1751. Kingston is the large city that sprang up to replace Port Royal, Jamaica after the terrible earthquake in the late seventeenth century. Kingston is now the capital, but in the eighteenth century the capital was Spanish Town with its handsome public buildings, some of which were probably designed by Peter Harrison.

1-8	1s cast off in 8 counts (2s move up on counts 5–8) and dance two changes of rights & lefts.
9-16	Take hands on the sides and set twice, then 2 changes of rights & lefts.
17-24	1s and the couple below circle to the left and circle back to the right.
25-32	1s and 2s dance rights & lefts, four changes, starting with partners facing.

A TRIP TO MARTINIQUE
40-bar triple-minor longways; moderate-difficult.
dance & tune: Thompson II.

1-8	1s set twice to 2 woman and circle with her once around.
9-16	1s repeat with 2 man.
17-24	1s cast off in 8 counts (2s move up on counts 5–8) and circle to the left once around with the 3s.
25-32	Take hands along the lines and set twice; 1s circle once around to the left with the 2s.
33-40	1s lead out at the sides (lead out between 2 & 3 women, separate and cast in around the ends ; lead out between 2 & 3 men, separate and cast in around ends to progressed places proper).

A TRIP TO QUEBEC
32-bar triple or duple-minor longways; moderate.
dance & tune: Thompson II.

1-8	1s cross & cast, and turn once around with 2 hands in 4 counts, ending improper, then repeat to below the next couple, ending proper.
9-16	1s dance quickly half a figure-8 up through the couple above in 4 counts, set, then complete the figure-8 and set again.
17-24	1s lead up the middle to original places in 8 counts, set and cast off (2s move up).
25-32	All 3 couples circle to the left and circle back to the right.

151

A TRIP TO RICHMOND I
32-bar duple-minor longways; moderate.
dance & tune: Johnson V & Walsh 1750. The Richmond here is probably Richmond, Yorkshire or the Richmond that was once a village up the Thames River from London (now part of London), rather than Richmond, Virginia, which was founded in 1737, but since the Virginia city was founded by William Byrd II, who was very well connected in England, it is possible that the dance does refer to the Virginia city.

1-8	1 man turn 2 woman once around by the right, then his partner by the left.
9-16	1 woman turn 2 man once around by the left, then her partner by the right.
17-24	1s cross & cast (2s move up) and dance half a figure-8 up through the 2s.
25-32	1s and 2s dance rights & lefts, four changes, starting with partners facing.

A TRIP TO RICHMOND II
32-bar triple or duple-minor longways; moderate-difficult.
dance & tune: Thompson II. Richmond, Virginia was named for the family of the Duke of Richmond, friends of William Byrd II. The Duke lost at gambling and was forced to marry his son to the winner's daughter, both being about 12 years old. The pair were separated for their education and when young Richmond went to the opera in London after having been abroad for a long time, he instantly fell in love with a lady he spotted on the other side of the theatre. He asked who she was and was told she was his wife! They lived happily ever after. Young Richmond served as head of the Royal Navy and then resigned because he opposed the new government's policy towards America.

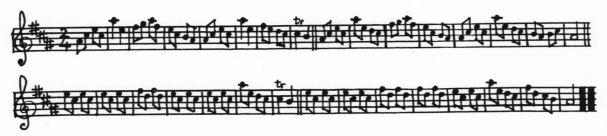

1-8	1s cast off and cross over while going down the middle one more place; cast up one place and cross over while going up the middle to original places.
9-16	1s cross & dance down the outside for 8 counts to below 2 standing couples, dance up the middle while crossing over to proper sides and fall into progressed places (2s having moved up).
17-24	1s lead down through the couple below and cast up again; lead up through the couple above and cast down again.
25-32	1s circle to the left once around with the couple below, then dance quick rights & lefts with the couple above (2 counts per side).

A TRIP TO SAINT GEORGE'S

32-bar triple-minor longways; moderate-difficult.
dance & tune: Johnson, 1751. Saint George's is the original capital of Bermuda, where the world's oldest legislature building can still be visited.

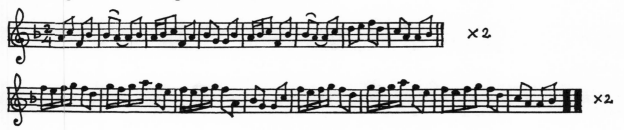

1-8	Partners set and change sides, set and change back again.
9-16	1s cross & dance down the outside for 8 counts to below 2 standing couples, dance up the middle while crossing over to proper sides and fall into progressed places (2s having moved up).
17-24	1s set to first corners and turn them once around with 2 hands in 4 counts, then set to and turn second corners.
25-32	1s lead up to the top, crossing to proper sides, and cast off; lead down through the 3s and cast back up.

A TRIP TO THE JERSEYS

32-bar triple-minor longways; moderate.
dance & tune: Skillern, 1780.

1-8	The three men circle to the left once around in 8 counts and circle back to the right, while the three women lead counterclockwise around the men to places.
9-16	The three women circle to the left and circle back to the right, while the three men lead clockwise around the women to places.
17-24	1s go down the middle, come back and cast off (2s moving up).
25-32	All 3 couples circle to the left and circle back to the right.

A TRIP TO THE JUBILEE

16-bar duple-minor longways in 9/8 slipjig) time; difficult.
dance & tune: Playford, 1703; Feuillet/Essex, 1710. Since the word jubilee means the celebration of the 25th anniversary of some event, it is difficult to find any important event to which the title refers.

1-8

1s cross over by right shoulders and turn single to the left (all in 6 counts) while the 2s wait 3 counts and cross over in 3 counts; all face out; all lead out 3 counts and back in 3 counts; 1s take both hands and slip down one place in 3 counts while the 2s slip up the outside; all turn single cloverleaf; partners turn half way around by the right and fall back.

9-16

"Run-around:" 2s cast and lead up while 1s lead up and cast off, all in 9 counts; partners turn once and a quarter by the right so as to slide into a single line with back to partner (men face up, women face down); balancer to the right, then the left and turn single out to progressed places.

A TRIP TO VIRGINIA

32-bar triple or duple-minor longways; moderate.
dance & tune: Johnson.

1-8   Partners set and change sides, set and change back again.

9-16   1s cross & cast and lead down through the couple below, cast up to progressed places (2s move up) and turn half way around with 2 hands.

17-24   1s set to first corners and turn them once around with 2 hands in 4 counts, then set to and turn second corners.

[in a duple-minor version, all should dance with the person diagonally on the right for "first corners" and the person diagonally on the left for "second corners".]

25-32   All 3 couples circle to the left and circle back to the right.

TWENTY-ONE

32-bar duple-minor longways; moderate.
dance & tune: Frobischer MS.

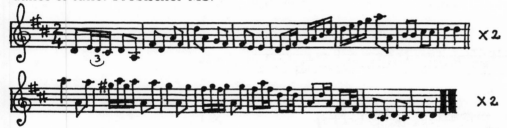

1-8	1s turn once and a half times around by the right and cast off.
9-16	1s turn one and a half times around by the left and cast back up.
17-24	1s go down the middle, come back and cast off (2s moving up).
25-32	1s and 2s dance rights & lefts, four changes, starting with partners facing.

VALENTINE'S DAY

28-bar duple-minor longways improper; moderate.
dance & tune: Playford 4th edition, 1670; dance in A New Academy, 1795.

the 1s improper

1-8	Partners take near hands; 1s (improper) lead up a double while 2s lead down a double; change hands and lead back; neighbors lead out a double, change hands and lead back.
9-18	Women corners cross; men corners cross; neighbors take hands and fall back a double, then come forward, cross over, changing places with partner to progressed places.
19-28	Women corners dance into the center and stand with backs to each other and clap; men corners do likewise; all clap four times while turning single to the right into a slipping circle to the left to fall back into progressed places.

LA VAUDREUIL LONGWAYS
40 or 32-bar triple or duple-minor longways; moderate.
dance: Fraisier, The Scholar's Companion, 1796; tune: American MS, ca.1800.

1-8	1s set twice to the 2 woman, then all 3 dance a right-hand star.
9-16	1s set twice to the 2 man, then all 3 dance a left-hand star.
17-24	1s go down the middle, come back and cast off (2s moving up).
25-32	Partners allemande right and fall back; take hands with neighbors and dance forward a double (with contretemps step) and back.
33-40	1s and 2s dance rights & lefts, four changes, starting with partners facing.

THE VIRGINIA REEL OF 1809
32-bar triple-minor (or 3-couple set) longways; moderate.
dance: Wilson, Treasures of Terpsichore, 1809; tune: use any lively 32-bar reel or hornpipe. This dance was not published until well into the nineteenth century, but it is likely to date from the eighteenth century. It is merely one of many dances that were described at the time as Virginia Reels; perhaps the term meant any dance with reels of some sort in it that was not a Scots foursome reel. See also the page with Trenchmore.

1-8	1s go down the outside for 8 counts, turn and come back.
9-16	1s go down the middle, come back and cast off (2s moving up).
17-24	1s and 2s dance rights & lefts, four changes, starting with partners facing.
25-32	1s turn first corners once around with 2 hands, then turn second corners once around with 2 hands.

THE WALTON

32-bar duple-minor longways; moderate.
dance & tune: Cantelo,   1785, written by "Capt.W."

1-8	1s promenade counterclockwise around the 2s; then the 2s promenade clockwise around the 1s.
9-16	1s go down the middle, come back and cast off (2s moving up).
17-24	1s and 2s dance rights & lefts, four changes, starting with partners facing.
25-32	Partners allemande right and then allemande left.

WASHINGTON FOR EVER

32-bar triple-minor longways; moderate.
dance: Griffiths II, 1794; tune: General Washington's March, Murphey MS, 1790.

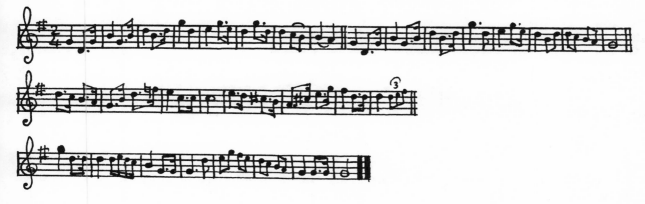

1-8	Partners set and change sides by the right, then set and change back again by the left.
9-16	1s go down the middle, come back and cast off (2s moving up).
17-24	1s turn first corners once around with 2 hands, then turn second corners once around with 2 hands.
25-32	Men face down and women face up; all chasser 4 steps across the set (partners passing face to face); rigadoon, chasser back and rigadoon.

WASHINGTON'S RESIGNATION
32-bar triple-minor longways; moderate.
dance: Griffiths I, 1788; tune: Turner MS.

1-8   Partners set and change sides by the right, then set and change back again by the left.

9-16   1s go down the middle, come back and cast off (2s moving up).

17-24   All 3 couples circle to the left and circle back to the right.

25-32   1s lead out at the sides (lead out between 2 & 3 women, separate and cast in around the ends ; lead out between 2 & 3 men, separate and cast in around ends to progressed places proper).

WE'LL WED & WE'LL BED
12-bar (in 12/8 time) or 24 bars (in 6/8 time) duple-minor longways; moderate.
dance & tune: Playford vol.II. This dance was renamed Dublin Bay in the 20th century, when it was worked out (the original is full of typographical errors).

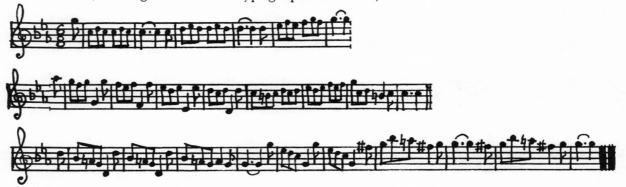

1-14
1s cross as they set to their corners (1 woman passing ahead of her partner) and turn corners once around by the right; 1s cross above the 2s by left shoulders and cast; dance up between the 2s to face neighbor; neighbors arm right once around (some people do it several times around, but be careful not to hurt anyone; at least one broken arm has resulted from this); end in line across, facing down, with 1s in the middle.

15-24
Lines fall back a double, come forward a double and turn individually to face up; new lines fall back a double and come forward; 1s cast off with assistance from 2s.

THE WELCH QUESTION
32-bar duple-minor longways; moderate.
dance & tune: Young's Vocal etc. Miscellany, Philadelphia, 1793. The word Welch is the 18th-century spelling of Welsh.

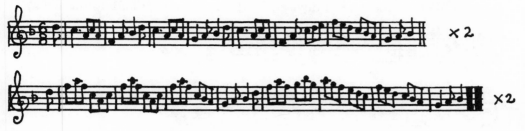

1-8	Second corners turn once and a half around with 2 hands to change places; first corners do likewise.
9-16	Repeat back to places.
17-24	1s go down the middle, come back and cast off (2s moving up).
25-32	1s and 2s dance rights & lefts, four changes, starting with partners facing.

WELCOME FROM THE HAVANA
24-bar duple-minor longways; moderate.
dance & tune: Thompson, 1773.

1-8	1s and 2s dance a right-hand star and a left-hand star back.
9-16	1s cross & cast (2s move up) and dance half a figure-8 up through the 2s.
17-24	1s and 2s dance rights & lefts, four changes, starting with partners facing.

THE WET QUAKERS

32-bar triple-minor longways; moderate.

dance & tune: Bride, ca.1782. Quakers were occasionally found in England, but they were far more numerous in Pennsylvania, whence British troops had evacuated only shortly before this dance was published. Therefore, this dance is likely to have been devised by the British in Philadelphia in 1777.

1-8	Partners set and change sides by the right, then set and change back again by the left.
9-16	1s go down the middle, come back and cast off (2s moving up).
17-24	1s turn first corners by right hands, turn partner by the left.
25-32	1s turn second corners by right hands, turn partner by the left.

THE WHIMSICAL LADY

32-bar triple or duple-minor longways; moderate.

dance: Griffiths I, 1788; tune, The Whimsical Lover, Nivison MS.

1-8	Partners turn by the right, then turn by the left.
9-16	1s go down the middle, come back and cast off (2s moving up).
17-24	1s turn first corners once around with 2 hands, then turn second corners once around with 2 hands.
25-32	Whole poussette clockwise.

THE WILLING QUAKER

32-bar duple-minor longways; moderate.

dance & tune: Thompson, 1780. Like The Wet Quakers, this dance is likely to have been devised by the British at Philadelphia about 1777; since Quakers were not supposed to dance (although some did so anyway), the British no doubt drew humor from including the word Quaker in dance titles.

1-8	1s and 2s dance a right-hand star and a left-hand star back.
9-16	1s go down the middle, come back and cast off (2s moving up).
17-24	1s and 2s circle to the left and circle back to the right.
25-32	Partners allemande right and then allemande left.

THE YAGER [sic JAEGER] HORN

32-bar triple-minor longways; moderate.

dance & tune: Cantelo, 1785. The Jaegers were the German mercenary equivalents of the Rangers, soldiers equipped with rifles and skilled in the lore of the wilderness. Like other huntsmen, Jaegers no doubt blew horns while hunting deer, boar or fox.

1-8	1s circle to the left once around with the 2 woman; then 1s circle with the 2 man, leaving 1 man standing between the 3s, while 1 woman stands between the 2s.
9-16	Taking hands in lines of 3 across the set, all set twice; 1s turn by the right to return to proper sides in 2nd place.
17-24	All 3 couples taking hands on the sides set twice and then partners turn with 2 hands once around.
25-32	All 3 couples circle to the left and circle back to the right.

YORK FUSILIERS

32-bar triple or duple-minor longways; moderate.

dance: Griffiths II, 1794; tune: Murphey MS. The tune was a popular march played on the fifes of both British and American units in the War of Independence.

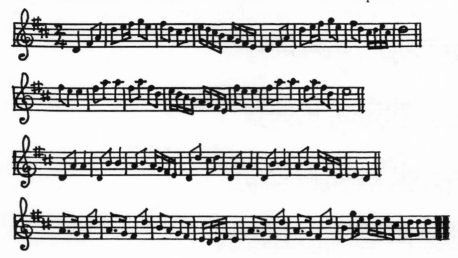

1 & 2 men make an arch and cross to women's side while the 1 & 2 women go under the arch to the men's side; changing hands, the men make an arch and cross back while the women go under the arch to return to places.

1s go down the middle, come back and cast off (2s moving up).

1s turn first corners once around with 2 hands, then turn second corners once around with 2 hands.

1s lead out at the sides (lead out between 2 & 3 women, separate and cast in around the ends ; lead out between 2 & 3 men, separate and cast in around ends to progressed places proper).

COTILLIONS

THE ACADEMY COTILLION
cotillion with 32-bar chorus; moderate.
dance: Griffiths I, 1788; tune: Alliance Cotillion, Carroll MS.

1-8
Form 2 longways lines (between heads), take hands along the lines and set; pattacake with opposite.
Repeat.

9-16
In groups of 4, poussette clockwise half way around; chasser back again (women going in front of men); turn single cloverleaf and fall back into the square.

17-32
Women set twice; rights & lefts, 2 changes; set twice; rights & lefts 2 changes home.

L'ALLEMANDE COTILLION (The German Lass)
cotillion with 32 or 64-bar chorus; moderate.
dance & tune: Trois Rivières MS, ca.1765; tune completed by Ticknor & Millar.

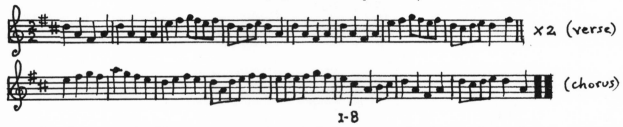

x2 (verse)

(chorus)

1-8

Heads advance a double (contretemps step); balancer or rigadoon; chain the women across; men promenade that woman around inside of set in overhead allemande position.

9-16

Repeat back to places.

ALLEMANDE SUISSE COTILLION (German-speaking Swiss Lass)
cotillion with 16 or 32-bar chorus; moderate.
dance & tune: Trois Rivières MS, ca.1765; alternate dance, early American MS.

x2 (verse)

(chorus)

Canadian version   1-8

Heads promenade to the couple on their right; all rigadoon; leaving the first side couple, heads continue promenading around to meet the other side couple; all rigadoon.

9-16

Right-hand star with this couple; allemande-left with opposite back to places.

U.S. version   1-8

Heads face couple on the right; all set once moving forward, and fall back; opposites change places by right shoulders and turn back to face opposite.

9-16

Opposites allemande-right once and a half around; partners allemande-left once around back to places.

164

LE BALLET DES MANSEAUX COTILLION/LE CHÂTEAU DU LOY

cotillion with **32**-bar chorus; moderate.
dance & tune: Trois Rivières MS, ca.1765; tune completed by Ticknor & Millar.

x2 (verse)

(chorus)

1-8

Heads advance & retire; sides advance & retire.

9-16

All chasserto far corners (woman passing in front of partner); rigadoon; allemande-right once around.

17-24

All chasser back to places and face near corner; rigadoon & allemande-right once around.

25-32

Grand chain all around (starting with partners facing), with a balancer each time partners meet.

LA BARONNE COTILLION (The Baroness)

cotillion with **32**-bar chorus; moderate.
dance: Trois Rivières MS, ca.1765; tune: Contre Danse, Quebec Seminary MS.

x2 (verse)

(chorus)

1-8

Head women chain across while sides chasser out and back. Heads stand between the nearest sides in lines of 4; lines advance & retire.

9-16

Head men face side woman on right and begin a chain that brings heads back to places.

LA BEAUTÉ COTILLION (The Beauty)
cotillion with 32-bar chorus; moderate.
dance: Griffiths I, 1788; tune: Perkins MS.

1-8

All chasser to far corners, balancer and turn once around with 2 hands.

9-16

Men weave around set counterclockwise, starting by passing first woman by the right.

17-24

Partners balancer, rigadoon and turn once around with 2 hands.

25-32

Women form right-hand star, holding onto partner's hand with the left, and move the giant star around back to places.

LES BOIS COTILLION (The Woods)
cotillion with 16 or 32-bar chorus; moderate.
dance: Trois Rivières MS, ca.1765; tune: Contre Danse, Quebec Seminary MS.

1-8

Each head dances past (outside) his/her corner to stand between the side couples in lines of 4 on the sides; lines advance & retire.

9-16

Heads dance right-hand star and circle to the right back to places, WHILE sides chasser to side person of opposite sex not their partner, rigadoon, chasser back & rigadoon.

LE CERCLE/LE CERCEAU COTILLION (The Hoop)
cotillion with 32-bar chorus; moderate.
dance & tune: Trois Rivières MS, ca.1765; tune completed by Ticknor & Millar.

1-8

Heads advance & retire; sides advance & retire.

9-16

All chasser to far corners, rigadoon, chasser back & rigadoon.

17-24

All promenade counterclockwise around to opposite places; partners turn once around by the right.

25-32

Partners turn once around by the left and continue the promenade around to places.

THE CHARLOTTE COTILLION
cotillion with 16-bar chorus; moderate to easy.
dance: Griffiths I, 1788; tune: The Royal Charlotte, Thompson, 1765.

1-8

Women promenade clockwise in an inner circle for 8 counts WHILE men promenade counterclockwise in an outer circle; partners balancer & rigadoon.

9-16

Repeat back to places.

THE COLLY FLOWER COTILLION (sic, Cauliflower)
cotillion with 24-bar chorus; moderate.
dance: Bourne, early 19th-c. imprint; tune: Skipwith MS (VA), ca.1790.

Heads   1-8
Partners face and dance forward a double & back and turn once around with 2 hands.
                                    9-16
The 1 woman join the opposite couple in a line of 3 with man in the middle (next time around, the 2 woman, etc.); those 3 dance forward a double to her partner and back; then he sets twice to them.
                                    17-24
Those same 4 circle once around to the left; partners turn once around with 2 hands to places.

COLUMBUS COTILLION
cotillion with 16 or 32-bar chorus; moderate.
dance & tune: Bourne, early 19th-c. imprint; perhaps actually written 1792 to celebrate the 300th anniversary of Columbus' voyage.

Heads dance 2 changes of rights & lefts; all chasser to far corners and chasser back.
99
Heads dance 2 changes of rights & lefts back; partners balancer and turn quickly around with 2 hands.

168

THE CONSTITUTION COTILLION

cotillion with 16-bar chorus; moderate.
dance: Saltator I, 1802; tune: 18th-c. American MS; probably written in honor of the ratification of the Constitution of the United States in 1788.

1-8

Heads set twice, moving forwards, and do a right-hand star half way around, ending in opposite places, WHILE the sides dance half way around the outside of the set (Men going counterclockwise and Women going clockwise), take two hands and rigadoon when they meet.

9-16

Then all repeat the figure back to original places, the sides doing what the heads did and vice versa.

LA DAME FRANÇOISE COTILLION (The French Lady)

cotillion with 24-bar chorus; moderate-easy.
dance: Trois Rivières MS, ca.1765; tune: Beck MS.

1-8

Heads advance & retire WHILE sides chasser out & back; then sides advance & retire WHILE heads chasser out & back.

9-16

Starting by going in front of their corner, women weave the ring completely around the set.

17-24

Starting by going in front of their corner, men weave the ring completely around the set.

LA DÉLICE COTILLION (The Delight)
cotillion with 56-bar chorus; moderate.
dance: Griffiths I, 1788; tune: Turner MS.

×2 (verse)

(chorus)

1-8

Heads lead forward a double, then lead opposite out a double to the side; turn opposite half way around by the right and back by the left, returning home.

9-16

Sides do what heads did.

17-24

Heads change places with opposites and turn partner once around with 2 hands.

25-32

Sides do what heads did.

33-48

Repeat back to places.

49-56

Take hands in a circle, chasser 8 steps to the left and 8 back to the right.

THE FEDERAL COTILLION
cotillion with 32-bar chorus; moderate.
dance & tune: American imprint, ca.1790.

×2 (verse)

(chorus)

(honors)

1-8

Heads advance & retire and dance 2 changes of rights & lefts.

9-16

Sides do what heads did.

17-24

All circle to the left and circle back to the right.

25-32

Men dance a right-hand star half way around, give left to opposite woman to put her into a star half way around; men give left to partner to bring her to place.

33-34

Partners honor.

170

THE FEDERATION COTILLION
cotillion with 24-bar chorus; moderate.
dance & tune: Roth MS, 1790s.

x 2   (verse)

(chorus)

1-8

Head men chasser to the right 4 steps while head women chasser to the left; rigadoon; chasser back; rigadoon.

9-16

Heads dance a right-hand star and a left-hand star back.

17- 24

Partners balancer twice; heads dos-à-dos with opposite.

THE FORTY-SECOND [REGIMENT] COTILLION
cotillion with 16-bar chorus; moderate.
dance: Griffiths I, 1788; tune: Shepherd MS; the tune is also known to fifers as Garb of Old Gaul.

X 1 (verse)

(chorus)

Heads lead forward a double to face the couple on the left; those couples facing take hands in circles of 4, set, chasser 4 steps to the left and 4 back to the right.

Partners set, turn once around by the right hand to places and balancer.

GEORGE WASHINGTON'S FAVOURITE COTILLION

cotillion with 32 or **16**-bar chorus; moderate.
dance: early American; tune: Hurlbert; the tune appears in Thompson under the name of Midnight Ramble.

x2 (verse)

(chorus)

1-8

Heads face partners and step back while sides move in to form lines of 4 on the sides; chasser 4 steps on the sides (2 woman & 1 man and 4 woman & 3 man take hands and chasser left in front of others who chasser right) and balancer; make 2 right-hand stars and turn them around half way.

9-16

Same people chasser on the sides again and balancer; make 2 circles and circle to the left half way around to places.

Note: this is a condensation of the original instructions, which include 4 chassers instead of 2 and stars in both directions and circles in both directions—it takes hours to do!

THE HAPPY MEETING COTILLION

cotillion with 32-bar chorus; moderate.
dance: Griffiths I; tune: Thompson.

x2 (verse)

(chorus)

1-8

Heads set, moving forwards, take near hands with opposite and lead out the sides, the side partners separating to allow them to pass; heads separate and cast back to places.

9-16

Sides do what heads did.

17-24

All chasser to far corners, rigadoon and turn once around with 2 hands.

25-32

All chasser back, face near corners, rigadoon and turn once around with 2 hands.

LA HOLLANDOISE COTILLION (The Dutch Lass)
cotillion with 32-bar chorus; moderate.
dance: Trois Rivières MS, ca.1765; tune: Turner MS.

×2 (verse)

(chorus)

1-8

Heads advance a double to the sides on their right; all rigadoon; heads continue a double around the set to the other sides; all rigadoon.

9-16

Heads right-hand star once around and circle to the right back to places.

LA JEUNESSE COTILLION (Youthfulness)
cotillion with 48-bar chorus; moderate.
dance: Griffiths I, 1788; tune: Fishar.

× (verse)

(chorus)

1-8

Heads set, rigadoon and turn opposite once around with 2 hands.

9-16

Sides do what heads did.

17-24

All chasser to far corners, rigadoon and turn once around with 2 hands.

25-32

All chasser back, face near corners, rigadoon and turn once around with 2 hands.

33-40

Form lines on the sides, set, rigadoon and dance two right-hand stars once around.

41-48

Repeat with left-hand stars to places.

LA JOLIE COTILLION (The Pretty Lass)
cotillion with 32-bar chorus; moderate.
dance & tune: Trois Rivières MS, ca.1765; tune completed by Ticknor & Millar.

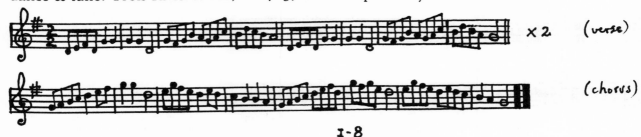

1-8

All chasser to far corners, rigadoon, chasser back & rigadoon.

9-16

Grand chain half way around, starting with partners facing; partners turn once around with 2 hands.

17-24

All chasser to far corners, rigadoon, chasser back & rigadoon.

25-32

Grand chain half way around, starting with partners facing; partners turn once around with 2 hands.

LES JOLIES DAMES COTILLION (The Lovely Ladies)
cotillion with 24-bar chorus; moderate.
dance: Griffiths I, 1788; tune: Lovely Nymph, Perkins MS.

1-8

Heads lead forward a double to the couple on the right, balancer, rigadoon and 1/4 poussette to change places with that couple.

9-16

All repeat the figure back to original places, the sides doing what the heads did and vice versa.

17-24

All circle to the left and circle back to the right.

LAFAYETTE COTILLION
cotillion with 24-bar chorus; moderate.
dance: Griffiths I, 1788; tune: Adams MS.

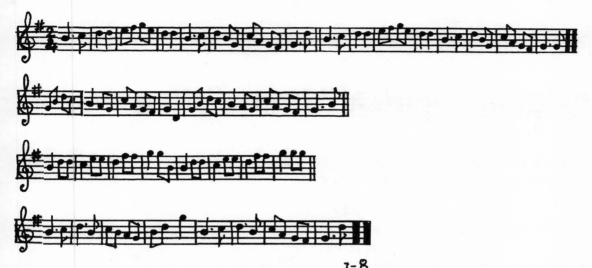

1-8

Heads divide and dance a right-hand star with their corners once around and a left-hand star back.

9-16

Heads and the couple on their left advance and change places by right shoulders in 4 counts, set, advance and change with the next couple and set.

17-24

Partners face and dance rights & lefts back to places.

LA MODE À L'ENVER COTILLION (The Style on the Wrong Side)
cotillion with 64-bar chorus; moderate.
dance & tune: Trois Rivières MS, ca.1765; tune completed by Ticknor & Millar.

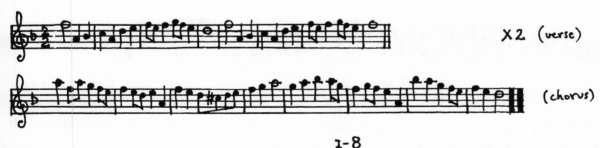

X2 (verse)

(chorus)

1-8

Heads advance & retire; advance again and change places by right shoulders.

9-16

Sides do what heads did.

17-32

Repeat back to places.

33-64

Then head men (without changing places) take their corners and do likewise [this part involving corners could be made the chorus of alternate verses if desired].

Then side men do likewise with their corners.

LA NOUVELLE BOHÉMIENNE COTILLION (The New Bohemian Girl)
cotillionwith **24** or 48-bar chorus; moderate.
dance & tune: Trois Rivières MS, ca.1765; tune completed by Ticknor & Millar.

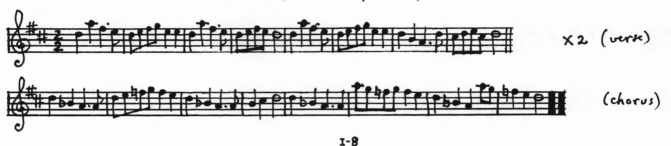

x2 (verse)

(chorus)

1-8

Heads promenade in overhead allemande position clockwise around the outside to opposite places, do a 4-count overhead-allemande and return to places through the middle, passing right shoulders with opposites.

9-16

Head women chain across and chain back.

17-24

Heads face couple on the right and take hands in a ring; chasser 4 steps to the left and back to the right. Heads shake right index finger twice at opposite, clap hands twice and return home in overhead allemande position.

LA NOUVELLE MAHONNE COTILLION/LE RICHELIEU
cotillion with 16 bar-chorus; moderate.
dance & tune: Trois Rivières MS

x2 (verse)

(chorus)

1-8

All chasser to far corners 4 steps and turn once around in 4 counts with 2 hands; dance two right-hand stars once around (one star on either side of the axis between head places).

9-16

Chasser back to regular corners and turn once around in 4 counts with 2 hands; dance two right-hand stars as before.

LA NOUVELLE ROYALLE COTILLION (The New Princess Royal)

cotillion with 16 or 32-bar chorus; moderate.
dance & tune: Trois Rivières MS, ca.1765; tune completed from tune of same name in Wright.

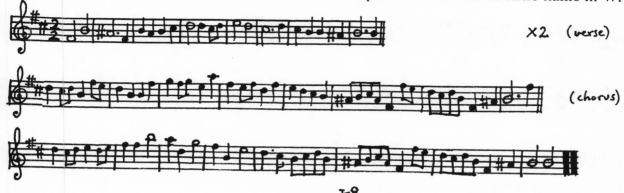

1-8
All women advance with 2 balancers, rigadoon and turn single.

9-16
All women dance a right-hand star for 6 counts, then circle back to the right in 6 counts; partners overhead allemande to places in 4 counts.

17-32
Men do what women did.

OPEN THE DOOR TO THREE or WINIFRED'S KNOT

three verses each 36 bars in 6/8 time or 24 bars in 9/8 (slipjig) time, four-couple round or square set
dance & tune: Playford II, 1652; tune in Turner MS, 1786–8.

First Verse
All take hands and slip eight slips clockwise, then turn single.
Slip back eight slips counter-clockwise, then turn single.

Chorus
The Men move forward a double to the center and fall back again to places. Then each man passes the woman on his left by right shoulders and arrives in the next man's place. This figure is repeated until all the men have travelled completely around the set clockwise. The chorus for the second verse differs in that it is the Women who are active, and they pass the men by left shoulders going counter-clockwise.

Second Verse
Partners side to right shoulders, then turn single.
Partners side to left shoulders, then turn single.
  Women's chorus.

Partners arm right, then turn single.
Partners arm left, then turn single.
  Men's chorus.

LES ORMEAUX COTILLION (The Young Elm Trees)
cotillion with 32-bar chorus; moderate.
dance & tune: Trois Rivières MS, ca.1765; tune completed by Ticknor & Millar.

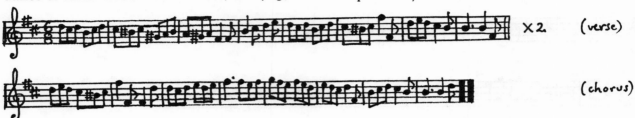

1-8

All chasser to far corners, balancer or rigadoon, chasser back and balancer or rigadoon.

9-16

Partners facing, grand chain half way around and rigadoon with partner.

17-32

Repeat to places.

LA PAISANNE DISSÉE COTILLION (The Gossipy Peasant Girl)
cotillion with 32-bar chorus; moderate.
dance & tune: Trois Rivières MS, ca.1765; tune completed by Ticknor & Millar.

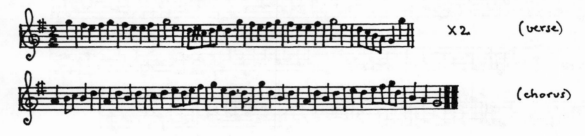

1-8

Heads dance rights and lefts.

9-16

Heads dance a right-hand star for 8 counts, then circle to the right back to places.

LES PANIERS COTILLION (The Baskets Cotillion)
cotillion with 24-bar chorus; moderate.
dance: Griffiths I, 1788; tune: published by Ditson, 19th c.

1-8
Heads turn single to the right to form a ring; chasser left for 4 counts and chasser back to the right; partners take near hands and balancer to opposites.

9-16
Head man change places with opposite; head woman change places with opposite; partners turn once around with 2 hands.

17-24
Head man balancer and 2-hand turn in 4 counts with opposite to change places; head woman and opposite do likewise.

LE PAPILLON/LES MARIONETTES COTILLION (The Butterfly or the Puppets)
cotillion with 32-bar chorus; moderate.
dance & tune: Trois Rivières MS, ca.1765; tune completed by Ticknor & Millar.

1-8
Each woman moves into the place of the woman on the right in 4 counts (turning single as she goes) and rigadoon; repeat to the next place.

9-16
Repeat the previous figure.

17-32
Men do what the women did, starting to the left and turning single to the left.

LE PETIT BALLET COTILLION/MAHON (The Little Ballet)

cotillion with 24 or 48-bar chorus; moderate.
dance: Trois Rivières MS, ca.1765; tune: Assheton MS; tune also known as Voulez-Vous Danser, Mademoiselle.

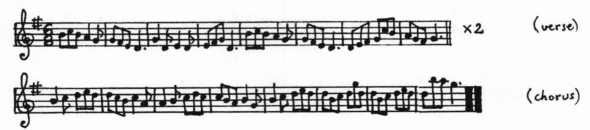

(verse)

(chorus)

1-8

Heads dance forward a double (contretemps step), rigadoon, and circle left for 8 counts.

9-16

Heads form an outward-facing circle and dance counterclockwise for 8 counts; each head man promenade his partner (with hand behind her back) counterclockwise around the inside of the set to places.

17-24

Heads dance rights & lefts, 4 changes.

LA PETITE ALLEMANDE COTILLION (The Little German Girl)

cotillion with 16 or 32-bar chorus; moderate.
dance & tune: Trois Rivières MS, ca.1765; tune completed by Ticknor & Millar.

(verse)

(chorus)

1-8

Heads take crossed hands, come forward a double (contretemps step) and rigadoon; still holding crossed hands, face about, dance forward a double (contretemps step) to places and rigadoon.

9-16

Corners allemande right; partners allemande left.

LA PETITE PAISANNE COTILLION (The Little Peasant Lass)
cotillion with 32-bar chorus; moderate.
dance & tune: Trois Rivières MS, ca.1765; tune completed by Ticknor & Millar.

1-8

Heads advance a double; in poussette hold, head men push opposite back to her place in 4 counts and turn once around with 2 hands.

9-16

Head men then push opposite woman around and back to the middle in 4 counts, so that she stands back to back with the other woman; heads rigadoon; head men pass opposite woman by left shoulder and loop around to meet partner and bring her home.

In the next chorus, the women push the men; each chorus alternates.

LA PETITE PROVINCE COTILLION (The Little State, meaning Rhode Island)
cotillion with 24-bar chorus; moderate.
dance: Griffiths I, 1788; tune: Rhode Island March II, Carroll MS.

1-8

Heads balancer and rigadoon, dance a right-hand star half way around and lead out to opposite places.

9-16

Sides do what heads did.

17-24

All promenade counterclockwise home in 8 counts; all chasser to far corners (woman passing in front) and back.

181

LA PIÈCE FUTOISE COTILLION (The Bit of Woodland)
cotillion with 16 or 32-bar chorus; moderate.
dance: Trois Rivières MS, ca.1765; tune: Turner MS.

1-8

Heads advance to couple on the right (ending with heads' backs to each other, but sides facing each other); all rigadoon; turn the person opposite half way around with 2 hands in 4 counts (ending with heads facing each other and sides' backs to each other); all rigadoon.

9-16

All return to places in 4 counts and rigadoon; partners allemande right.

LA PINTIÈVRE COTILLION (sic Penthièvre)
cotillion with 24-bar chorus; moderate.
dance & tune: Trois Rivières MS, ca.1765; the Duke of Penthièvre was one of the hereditary patrons of New France, to whom Father Charlevoix dedicated his 6-volume history of Canada in 1743.

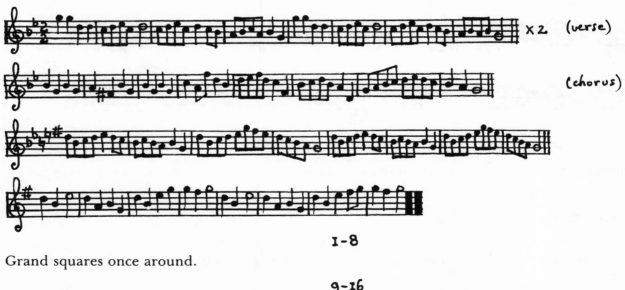

1-8

Grand squares once around.

9-16

Repeat back to places (reverse).

17-24

Heads dance a right-hand star once around and circle back to the right WHILE sides chasser to far corners, rigadoon, chasser back and rigadoon.

LA POLONAISE CONTREDANSE COTILLION (The Polish Country Dance)

cotillion with 32-bar chorus; moderate.
dance & tune: Trois Rivières MS, ca.1765; tune completed by Ticknor & Millar.

1-8

Heads chain the women across & back again.

9-16

heads dance a right-hand star once around and circle back to the right WHILE sides chasser to far corners, rigadoon, chasser back and rigadoon.

LA POUSSETTE COTILLION

cotillion with 16-bar chorus; moderate.
dance & tune: Trois Rivières MS, ca.1765; tune completed by Ticknor & Millar.

1-8

Partners take poussette hold; men push partners a double counterclockwise to the side, then a double to the left; she pushes him a double into the center and another double back to places.

9-16

Corners do what partners did.

QUEEN OF DIAMONDS COTILLION

cotillion with 16-bar chorus; moderate-easy.
dance: Blanchard, ca.1800; tune: by Henry Carey, The Musical Century II, 1740; Carey wrote the music for God Save the King.

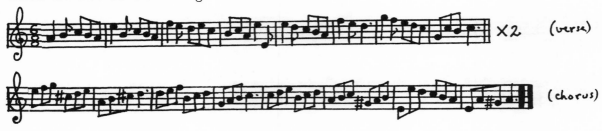

1-8

Partners take left hand in left; men turn women into a right-hand star; still holding hands, all balancer; then men drop hands and skip half way around the set counterclockwise WHILE the women move their star half way around.

9-16

Partners take left hand in left and change places, the men making a right-hand star; all balancer; then the men do what the women did and vice versa back to places.

LE RHINOCÉROS COTILLION

cotillion with 24 or 48-bar chorus; moderate.
dance & tune: Trois Rivières MS, ca.1765; tune completed by Ticknor & Millar.

1-8
Heads advance & retire; right-hand star half way around.
9-16
Heads promenade counterclockwise around the outside of the set to places in 12 counts and rigadoon.
17-24
Heads advance & retire; all chasser to far corners and back.

LA ROHANNE COTILLION

cotillion with 32 or 64-bar chorus; moderate.
dance & tune: Trois Rivières MS, ca.1765; tune is actually a Gavotte by Handel from his opera/oratorio Otho.

x2 (verse)

(chorus)

1-8

Heads advance & retire; all chasser to far corners and back.

9-16

Grand chain half way around, starting with partners facing; partners turn once around with 2 hands in 4 counts.

17-32

Repeat first 16 bars back to places.

LA TRACIE COTILLION

cotillion with 16 or 32-bar chorus; moderate.
dance: Griffiths I, 1788; tune: Carroll MS.

x2 (verse)

(chorus)

1-8

Heads change places with opposite by right shoulders in 8 counts; chasser across partner 4 steps and back.

9-16

Heads balancer & rigadoon; turn opposite once and a half around with 2 hands to places.

LA VAUDREUIL COTILLION

cotillion with 24 or 48-bar chorus; moderate.
dance: Fraisier, The Scholar's Companion, 1796; tune: New England MS, ca.1800; the Marquis de Vaudreuil ruled much of New France from his handsome palace in Montreal.

1-8

Head women chain across and back.

9-16

Heads separate and cast around to come in through side couples (who divide to let them pass), meet and return to places; then heads separate and form 2 right-hand stars on the sides and go once around.

17-24

The same couples who did the stars now dance rights & lefts, 4 changes, back to places.

LES VIGNOBLES À MARTIN COTILLION (The Vineyards at Martin)

cotillion with 24-bar chorus; moderate.
dance & tune: Trois Rivières MS, ca.1765; tune completed by Ticknor & Millar.

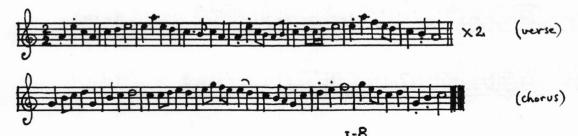

1-8

Heads advance & retire WHILE the sides chasser to far corners and back; all partners allemande right.

9-16

Sides do what heads did.

17-24

Women (taking partner's right hand in their left hand) make a right-hand star; the giant star dances half way around in 8 counts; partners continue a promenade back to places.